Expand your notion of reality!

Linda G Corley

For The Sake of My Country

An Intimate Conversation With Lt. Col. Jesse A. Marcel, Sr., May 5, 1981

Linda G. Corley, Ph.D.

AuthorHouse™
1663 Liberty Drive, Suite 200
Bloomington, IN 47403
www.authorhouse.com
Phone: 1-800-839-8640

AuthorHouse™ UK Ltd.
500 Avebury Boulevard
Central Milton Keynes, MK9 2BE
www.authorhouse.co.uk
Phone: 08001974150

© 2007 Linda G. Corley, Ph.D.. All rights reserved.

No part of this book may be reproduced, stored in a retrieval system, or transmitted by any means without the written permission of the author.

First published by AuthorHouse   1/25/2007

ISBN: 978-1-4259-8202-7 (sc)

Printed in the United States of America
Bloomington, Indiana

This book is printed on acid-free paper.

For The Sake Of My Country

Part One

An Intimate Conversation With Lt. Col. Jesse A. Marcel, Sr.

May 5, 1981

TABLE OF CONTENTS

TABLE OF FIGURES	5
PREFACE	9
INTRODUCTION	13
DEDICATION	19

CHAPTER ONE
A CITIZEN COMES FORTH	21
INTERVIEWS BY MEDIA	21
DEBRIS BROUGHT HOME	24
EVERYTHING NOT REVEALED	28
COVER UP BY AIR FORCE	31
BERMUDA TRIANGLE MYSTERY	32
FLYING COMBAT	35
HIEROGLYPHIC DRAWING	39

CHAPTER TWO
A PERSONAL THEORY OF UFOs	45
EXTRATERRESTRIAL TEACHERS	45
ALIEN AUTOPSY	48
FOURTH DIMENSION	49
THIRTY TWO YEAR SILENCE	52
HOLLYWOOD MOVIE OFFER	54
PROMOTION TO LT. COL.	58
COMMENDATION FROM NAVY	62
DESTINATION OF DEBRIS	65

CHAPTER THREE
A CUMULATIVE EFFECT OF EVENTS	69
AIR FORCE CAREER	69
AUTOBIOGRAPHY PLANNED	72
ZODIAC SIGNS	73
THE APPENDECTOMY	74
HYPNOTIC REGRESSION	75
DREAMS	80
HAM RADIO HOBBY	82

CHAPTER FOUR
A HOME REMEMBERED   85
   ROSWELL REVISITED   85
   DR. JESSE MARCEL JR.   87
   SPECIAL WEAPONS DEVELOPMENT   90

CHAPTER FIVE
A SANCTUARY FOR ALL   94
   CALVIN PARKER   94
   MEETING WITH PAUL WILMOT   96
   DESCRIPTION OF DEBRIS   99
   OTHER UFOs SIGHTED BY MARCEL   102
   NATIONAL SECURITY   104
   PHOTOS OF MARCELS TAKEN   108

CHAPTER SIX
A NEED FOR SOLITUDE   111
   HOLLYWOOD LIFE   111
   INTERNATIONAL GROUP ONE   112
   TELEPHONE INTERVIEWS   114

ANCIENT WRITING   117
   DEMOTIC HIEROGLYPHS   117
   TIRONIAN NOTES   119

FINAL THOUGHTS   127
BIBLIOGRAPHY   129

TABLE OF FIGURES

1.	Figure 1 Photo of Jesse in 1947	28
2.	Figure 2 Photo of General Ramey and Colonel DuBose	29
3.	Figure 3 Photo of Lt. Col. Payne Jennings	30
4.	Figure 4 Colonel Blanchard	31
5.	Figure 5 Jesse's Signed Drawing	40
6.	Figure 6 Photos of Marcel's House	75
7.	Figure 7 Photo of Jesse and Viaud	107
8.	Figure 8 Photo of Jesse and Viaud	107
8.	Figure 9 Photo of Jesse with author	108
9.	Figure 10 Demotic Hieroglyphs	116
10.	Figure 11 Tironian Notes	118
11.	Figure 12 Tironian Notes Block	118
12.	Figure 13 Beam	122
13.	Figure 14 Beam 2	122
14.	Figure 15 Beam 3	122

(Photo of Jesse Marcel in 1947 courtesy of the Forth Worth Star-Telegram Photograph Collection, Special Collections Division, University of Texas at Arlington Libraries.)

As the nuclear physicist who began the civilian investigation of the Roswell Incident and was first to talk about it to Jesse Marcel Sr, I am very pleased to see Linda Corley's interviews with him in print. He was a very special individual who served his country and his family well. We need more efforts like Linda's to solve the mystery of the strange symbols found and why Jesse didn't want her to use her interviews with him. We seem to know more about aliens than about the government's insistence on keeping facts secret.

~ STANTON T. FRIEDMAN

PREFACE

At an early age, I started my own serious study of the paranormal never knowing that later in life I would actually meet individuals who claimed to have had close encounters of the second, third, and fourth kind.

As a young teenage mother and housewife in the 1960s, I began reading books that were not ordinarily in my home library. I became engrossed in books that spoke of UFOs, cryonics, cloning, ESP, telepathy, clairvoyance, hypnosis, reincarnation, telekinesis, and other enigma and mysteries. I spent years reading about parapsychology even before it was recognized in 1969 by the American Association for the Advancement of Science.

I had an intense interest in becoming a Parapsychologist when I read about the work of Dr. Thelma Moss in California. How I longed to be able to study these fascinating subjects. However, there were no Universities near me that offered anything even close to this subject matter. So this passion was placed on the back burner and I discontinued my quest for knowledge on the subject and went on with my life. For approximately 10 years it appeared that I had lost interest in the study of the paranormal. I began traveling around the country and lived much of my life as a gypsy.

Then in the late 70s, while sitting on the banks of a Texas bayou fishing for food for my supper, I had an epiphany and the sudden urge to go home. Home to Louisiana. I was determined to change the course of my life and eventually enrolled in college. And of course, I majored in Psychology as this was the closest I could get to my true interests.

However, it was not until the book *The Roswell Incident* hit the stands that I decided to rekindle my love for books on the paranormal. In the spring of 1981, I checked this book out of the local library and once again my interest grew. I wondered how I would combine my studies of psychology with parapsychology. Then an idea suddenly came to me.

As a course assignment, I decided to interview interesting people and write reports to hand in as part of my academic requirements in Psychology. I immediately thought of the individual named in *The Roswell Incident* who just happened to live in my home town. I placed a call to the person named in the book, a Maj. Jesse Marcel, and requested an interview. He consented and a time and date were set.

The Marcels agreed to the use of a small tape recorder for the interview. I obtained three tapes of intimate conversation with the Marcels during that four hour interview. Most importantly, I was now in possession of a drawing Jesse did for me of what he remembered of the strange writing on the beams he found in the debris field. I was so excited about the possible academic grade that this report would surely bring me. Then the unexpected happened.

The day following the interview I returned to the Marcel home in order to give them copies of ancient writing which resembled what Jesse drew for me. Two days later, I received a phone call from Jesse. The voice at the other end of my phone was hysterical and threatening. It appeared that he did not want me to use the tapes for the school project or for anything else. This phone call was so upsetting to me that I put the tapes away and again placed a passion of mine on the back burner.

During the 1980s, I went on to devote most of my time to my academic endeavors and my career as a mental health counselor. After many years of dedication, I completed my undergraduate and graduate work in Psychology in 1986. I received my Ph.D. in Human Services in 1993.

With my education complete, I decided it was time to return to my first love - Parapsychology. Once again, I began reading books on the subject and concentrating on the latest findings concerning UFOs. This eventually led me back to the Marcel tapes.

It took 17 years for me to decide to transcribe the Marcel tapes for publication. There were several reasons why it took so long to make the decision. But the most important push to publish came from an acquaintance of mine in California, Ted Oliphant, who impressed on me the fact that I was holding a part of history all to myself. It is now my desire to give the reader my little part of history.

~~ LINDA G. CORLEY

INTRODUCTION

In the spring of 1981 I read the book *The Roswell Incident* by Charles Berlitz and William Moore which included the name and location of Major Jesse Marcel who was involved in the government cover up of a crashed UFO. Major Marcel was the intelligence officer for the 509th Composite Bomb Group of the Army Air Force stationed at Roswell, New Mexico. Major Marcel was a key witness and one of the first military personnel to handle the wreckage of a extraterrestrial spaceship crashed near Roswell in the early days of July 1947.

At the beginning of World War II, Roswell Army Airfield opened and became home to the 509th bombardment group. At one time the only Atomic Bomber wing in the world. Renamed Walker Air Force Base after the war, the airfield became a central part of the Strategic Air Command system.

The book answered a lot of questions for me, however, I had to know more about this Major Marcel. Ironically enough, he lived in Houma, Louisiana. This was my home town. I wondered if I could be so lucky as to be able to speak with him. After all, it would be as easy as dialing my neighbor. So, I phoned Major Marcel and requested an interview with him for a school project I was working on. I explained that I was a sophomore in college, majoring in Psychology, and the project included an interview with an interesting person of my choice. He invited me over on the afternoon of Tuesday, May 5, 1981 at 3:30 p.m. The interview took place at his kitchen table in his home located at 330 Skyline Drive, Bayou Blue, in Houma, Louisiana. His wife Viaud was the only other person present and participated in the discussion. They both agreed to the use of a tape recorder during the interview.

The meeting lasted for 4 hours and I can't remember a more pleasant and interesting visit. The Marcels lived in the country. Their home was serenely located among the trees indicative of the area. It sat at the end of a street lined with oak and pine trees, palmettos, and lots of green grass. There was a beautiful pond behind the house that actually had fish swimming around in it. I thought that this was just a little bit of heaven. I felt comfortable and was lavished with true Cajun hospitality during my visit there. I returned the next day, only briefly, to give the Marcels a drawing of Demotic Hieroglyphic writing, which Jesse was interested in seeing. When I left, there was an open invitation to return and visit whenever I wanted. I never saw the Marcels again.

Here we are in the new millennium, the year 2006. That was almost twenty five years ago, yet I can still hear Jesse's frantic voice on the telephone saying not to use any of the material obtained from my interview with him. He seemed almost hysterical when he called my home several days after the interview. He stated that everything he told me was a lie. I felt immediately that this was only his way of trying to prevent me from using the material, but I did not know why. I knew that most of what he told me had been previously published. My heart went out to him.

The second phone call was similar to the first. A day or so later he called to inquire if I had released any of the information. I assured him that it was only for a school project. But he insisted that I was going to the press with it. I tried to calm his fears and promised him that I would not use the information if he did not want me to. And for over a decade, I never did. The school project was never completed. For approximately 12 years the tapes sat on a shelf in my home. Not one person had ever heard the words Jesse and his wife spoke to me on that day in May.

When I read Jesse's obituary in the newspaper in 1986, I remembered how scared he sounded on that last phone call. I thought that now, finally, he didn't have anything more to fear from the incident at Roswell and that he had found peace. I felt that my promise to him had been kept. But as much as I wanted someone other than myself to hear the tapes, I could not bring myself to the point of releasing them. I feared that the tapes held some kind of information that

Jesse felt should not be made public. So more years went by and the tapes continued to sit on a shelf.

Then in 1993, 12 years after my interview with Jesse, I released the tapes to someone I felt would handle them in an appropriate way, someone that Jesse thought highly of. Stanton Friedman was that person. By this time, however, the tapes had become almost inaudible. If you knew Jesse and was able to understand him, through his coarse and gaspy voice due to emphysema, you could still only understand every other word on the tapes. Sadly, Stanton was unable to make out clearly what was being said in the interview. It seemed that I had waited too long.

Two of the tapes were returned to me in 1995 and the other in 1996 with hopes that I might be able to transcribe them. Stanton phoned me throughout this time, urging me to transcribe the tapes. The last time that I had listened to the tapes I had used the same recorder that was originally used during the interview. The same recorder that I used throughout my academic career. It was a very small portable cassette recorder used to record college lectures. I had long ago disposed of it and only recently purchased a new double cassette recorder and combination radio. This fact, as insignificant as it may sound, may be the only reason that a transcription was possible. Otherwise, the tapes may have been placed back on that shelf and never have been shared with anyone.

Throughout the years, since revealing the tapes to Stanton Friedman, I have received many calls from other interested parties. Each individual was courteous and requested permission to reveal my name and phone number to other researchers. I always agreed to this. Many are published authors on the subject. They all requested a copy of the transcription. I informed them that I could not give to one and not to another. And also, I was hesitant to reveal the contents because there was one other person to consider. Mrs. Marcel was still alive. I did not know what her feelings were on this matter but felt that I needed to protect her. She contributed to the interview in some very significant ways.

I guess the one statement that gave me the needed push to publish the manuscript came from an acquaintance who stated, "The information on the tapes is a part of history." And in that sense, I felt it needed to be made public. But did the personal issues, discussed during this conversation between the Marcels and myself, need to be made public? The relaxed talk over several glasses of wine could be too revealing. I was still struggling with that question.

In December of 1996, I decided to listen to the tapes one more time. Sitting at my kitchen table with my new cassette player I inserted tape number one. After several attempts at transcription, I was ready to give up. There was no way I was going to be able to transcribe this garbled conversation. In my frustration, I angrily pushed down on the play button and was taken back by the clear voice of Jesse Marcel coming through the player. I literally pushed away from the table with a jolt. The sound was so clear, it was like he was in the room with me.

The tapes had never been cleaned or enhanced in any way, nor did I know that this was possible. I am assuming that the new pads in this new recorder somehow cleaned the tape sufficiently for me to hear the words clearly.

This was the sign that I needed. This finally felt like the right thing to do. For the next 3 weeks I sat at that table every night and transcribed every word spoken during that four hour interview. And in doing so, went back in time. I laughed again with Jesse. I disagreed again with Jesse. I also enjoyed hearing this young, naive college student whose enthusiasm for life had since waned considerably over the years. Hearing her again was an inspiration. When the tedious task of transcription was over, I knew what I had to do. The only thing I could do. I decided to go public with the information.

UFO researchers still consider Roswell one of the most convincing UFO cases on record. I have read many books on the Roswell story and enjoyed movies based on the subject, but the story of Jesse Marcel the citizen, the actual story of his life, without embellishment or artistic liberty, would surely be intriguing entertainment within itself.

The very fact that this man not only touched what he believed to be a space craft not of this earth, but had pieces of it in his home, is utterly amazing to me. This was 1947. There were no television documentaries on UFO sightings as we have today. There were no support groups for people who claimed to have had a close encounter of some kind. How do you live your life after something like this happens to you? What coping mechanisms did the Marcels use throughout these years? What did Jesse believe that he didn't believe before the incident?

Whatever we may think of the incident at Roswell, whether we believe in UFOs and intelligent life on other planets or think it only science fiction, we cannot ignore the fact that the ability to seek our counterparts in the depths of space is now firmly in the realm of scientific reality today. Because of enormous technological strides made since the incident at Roswell, we are the first generation to pursue the adventure of exploration and the search for life among the stars. Let's hope we use it wisely.

Both to explain the reason for this publication and to justify some of the statements which appear herein, it is necessary for me to make this highly subjective statement. There are occasions, in the following pages, when serious UFO researchers may be offended by what strikes them as frivolous. Frivolity there may be but it should not be taken for disparagement of the field of UFOlogy in general or of particular researchers and their pet theories.

I follow the fairly conventional viewpoint which holds that events are the product both of THE MAN and THE BACKGROUND. I do believe that the shape of events is fashioned by the particular man who holds the reins of destiny at a particular moment in time. Any attempt to evaluate, or even describe, the character of a historical person is difficult and highly subjective.

Also, in my attempts to draw out the individual, often I inadvertently told more about myself than I may have wanted to. Please forgive me for that.

It is only fair to warn the reader that this is not a publication about the incident at Roswell but about a conversation with a man who took part in the incident at Roswell in 1947. My intention is to present an intimate conversation with Lt. Col. Jesse A. Marcel and his wife Viaud, word for word, and as best as I can remember. It is presented in interview format and I have noted the different inflections, emotions, and activities that took place during the interview. There are parts of the tapes that I was not able to clearly understand and have underlined these passages for the reader. Included are the photos of the Marcels and myself taken after the interview (see Figures 7 and 8) as well as the drawing Jesse did of a beam and the writings he saw on it. (See Figure 5)

DEDICATION

This book is dedicated to Lt. Col. Jesse A. Marcel Sr.

CHAPTER ONE
A CITIZEN COMES FORTH

> I held back with this premium for 32 years, without saying anything at all. Publicity is not what I want. I want peace.
>
> ~ JESSE MARCEL SR.

INTERVIEWS BY MEDIA

Jesse: I'm getting so sick and tired of getting calls from all over the country.

Linda: Are you? Oh, that's exciting. You should be excited.

Jesse: Not to me. For the past 2 years since the book was published...

Linda: Since that, huh? They are calling just to ask about the book and stuff like that?

Jesse: No. They want to know about me.

Linda: They want more about you personally?

Jesse: I've had people call me from all over the country. WGN TV in Chicago wanted to send a filming crew out here and interrogate me.

Linda Corley, Ph.D.

Linda: Really. That's good.

Jesse: They've gone too far. Spokane, Washington, they want to send a crew down here. I've entertained some of those before. One crew from Los Angeles... two crews from Los Angeles.

Linda: You granted them....? They came?

Jesse: Yeah. One crew from Los Angeles. I had to meet them in New Mexico to make the film out there.

Linda: They paid your way and everything?

Jesse: They paid my expenses. They didn't give me anything for my time.

Linda: Oh, but they paid for your expenses?

Jesse: Oh yeah. Same thing with WWL TV [New Orleans Station]. They paid all my expenses to New Mexico. We went out there. We filmed for two days... three days.

Linda: Is that what they're going to be showing this week on TV?

Jesse: Yeah, Johnny Mann [New Orleans TV reporter]. It might be on tonight. It will be on every night this week. In the news period, that's all you can get. He was on radio - WWL radio - yesterday all afternoon. He mentioned my name all over the place.

Linda: Well, did the people who've been calling you from all over the country ... you haven't been granting them ... you've been denying them [interviews]?

Jesse: I just give them a telephone interview, that's all.

Linda: Just a telephone interview, huh?

Jesse: The Washington Post called me. They wanted to run an article in the Washington Post magazine section. First of all, Bob Pratt of the National Inquirer came out here.

Linda: I can imagine they want to get something [from you].

Jesse: He spent two and a half hours here and he recorded a whole lot of stuff. What he was interested in was my military record. I showed him what I had and he read it.

Linda: But you should be proud of that. You're getting tired of it [attention from media]?

Jesse: Linda, I've had so much of it in my life that I just ... publicity is not what I want. I want peace.

[I think Jesse wanted peace from the secrets that he held of what happened at Roswell in 1947 and his role in the incident. He did not say this in so many words, but I feel that he had found peace in all other areas of his life. So why make this statement? He knew that there was not much time left in his life to close the door on that incident. But how do you go about closure on an event that your government said did not happen?]

Linda: Yeah, and you seem to have such a nice quiet place back here.

Jesse: Yeah, like Johnny Mann, he and his camera man came ever here. See, we filmed the scene in New Mexico at the site of the crash location. At the site. I took them there. All we did was a little walk out there. But we had a 45 mile per hour wind blowing. You couldn't record any sound.

Linda: So what did they do?

Jesse: They came back over here and I sat by the canal right back of my house and they did the recording here.

Linda: Oh, when is that going to be shown?

Jesse: Well, it will be in this series beginning tonight.

Linda: OK, and that's all you've done since the book has come out?

Jesse: Let's see. I know there is something else. I had an on-the-air telephone interview from New York City; on-the-air telephone interview from KTRS Houston. I'll tell you, they haven't left me alone.

Linda: You must have thought, "Here's another crazy person" calling you when I called, huh?

Jesse: No. Well after all, you were right here.

Linda: Yeah, well I'm so close. That's why I was so surprised that you lived so close.

DEBRIS BROUGHT HOME

Jesse: Hey, my son... Honey [speaking to wife], tell her about Jesse. They came over here to film our son. You see, our son was about eleven years old when I found all this stuff. And I was late coming home and I brought some of the stuff in the house where we lived in Roswell. Honey, you tell her.

Mrs. Marcel: No, you tell her.

Jesse: Anyway, we had a truck full. And I had a counter-intelligence agent working for me, you see. And I sent him to the base with the stuff. And I loaded my '42 Buick to the hilt with it and I came on home cause I was late getting home. She [wife] didn't even know where I was. By the time I got home, she had already faced the press that was out there. Oh, they told her that, "Your husband will make the world wide headline tomorrow." And I didn't even know that all that was happening. So when I got home, I brought some of the stuff and put it in the kitchen. My son, who was eleven years old, he was all ears and eyes. And so was she [Mrs. Marcel].

(Laughter) So I put a lot of stuff on the floor in the kitchen. One thing I don't remember is whether I picked it up or you [wife] and Jesse [junior] picked it up and put it back in my car. Cause I didn't get back to the base that night.

[The debris remained at his home overnight? If only he had taken some photos of the debris while it was in his possession. I know that he would not have kept any of the material because he was so loyal to the military, but some photos would have been a different story.]

Mrs. Marcel: All I remember is getting it out of my kitchen.

Linda: It was a mess?

Mrs. Marcel: It was a big mess. The kitchen was full of it.

Linda: I know the book [*The Roswell Incident*] said something about … you may have swept some out the back door and then they cemented over it.

Mrs. Marcel: I probably did [sweep some debris out the back door].

Linda: And they cemented the carport after that so we probably still have some [debris] somewhere in Roswell.

Mrs. Marcel: I would love to dig it up.

[This spontaneous remark by Mrs. Marcel was in agreement with speculation that there might still be remains of the debris, that is until Jesse hesitated then made the following remark.]

Jesse: I've been thinking back. We laid that cement before.

Mrs. Marcel: We had [laid cement] before that happened.

Jesse: Because we laid that cement just when I came back from the Atomic Bomb test in the Mid-Pacific in 1946 … this was 1947.

Linda Corley, Ph.D.

[What if this is still an attempt to keep a secret? If it were up to me, I would still dig up that cemented carport in Roswell.]

Linda: OK, so that's something. After you think about it for awhile you can remember better.

Jesse: Yeah, that's right. You know it's hard to remember the little details of everything that happened 33 years back.

Linda: You know, that's the year I was born. I was born the month after that happened, in August. August the second, 1947.

Jesse: Well, I can say you're not dry behind the ears then.

Linda: My moma said she feels that the UFOs brought me here. (Laughter)

Mrs. Marcel: Maybe they did. (Laughter)

Linda: It was the year that they were starting to sight them [UFOs] more. That … '47 was supposed to have been the first sighting here, so she said they must have brought me.

Jesse: Well, what happened to me, you see. When I found all this stuff and headquarters' 8th Air Force had squelched it … they put their foot on it … and I was told to keep my mouth shut. I held back with this premium for 32 years, without saying anything at all.

Linda: You didn't say anything for that long?

Jesse: That's right.

Mrs. Marcel: Well, of course not. I mean, when they [military] say don't do so and so, you don't.

[It can be noted throughout the interview that Mrs. Marcel would often validate Jesse's statements. I felt that this was an added indication that Jesse wasn't embellishing in order to impress a naive college student.]

Jesse: See, I was an intelligence officer. I had charge of intelligence and security for the base.

Linda: You had to set an example.

Jesse: In the meantime, I left the service but I still owed an allegiance to my country. To a vow that I took to keep my mouth shut about anything that might encroach on military secrets. Now this [UFO] could or couldn't. I don't know.

[This last statement was made reflecting the present time. I took this to mean that he still did not know whether or not this revelation could encroach on military secrets. I hesitated to ask Jesse why he had decided to speak out after all these years. I guess I just didn't want to ask an embarrassing question. He professed allegiance to his country, however, 32 years later he did, however, speak out on the military secrets that he was told not to do.]

Linda: You really didn't know then, if it was going to be any kind of military secret or anything like that?

[I was trying to establish whether or not he was referring to the past or present.]

Jesse: That's right. Well, obviously it proved to be because they're still sitting on it. They're not letting any information out on that. That's why I've been getting so many calls.

Linda: Yeah, so you think maybe that the book might help, maybe break through the barrier?

Jesse: I rather doubt it.

Linda: You don't think it's going to, huh?

Jesse: I'll tell you one thing. You have no idea how much I've been grilled. They want me to give them an opinion. Well, what is an opinion? An opinion, you can't prove factually. It's just an opinion. It's not worth anything. I can't prove factually because I've given away all the materials I had. Everything I picked up, the Air Force has it. They're still sitting on it.

Linda: But you saw it, though. That, they can't take from you. It's in your memory. Your mind still holds what you saw.

EVERYTHING NOT REVEALED

Jesse: All I can say is the material I picked up, I had never seen before 1947 and I haven't seen any of that material since 1947. What happened to it? The Air Force is still sitting on it.

Linda: What about … this was supposed to be like … the explosion supposedly had dropped this material and then supposedly the craft went over the mountain. Hasn't anything come up on this?

Jesse: They found a whole lot more of the same stuff about 80 miles to the southwest.

Linda: Supposedly another Air Force Base had taken care of that, huh?

Jesse: Well, I think once that happened … I think the military … See, they work like a network. They sent people all over the place. They gathered everything that was visible. So I just don't know. You see, all I know is what I did.

Linda: And what you were told after.

Jesse: And what I was told not to say. Which I'm still not saying.

Linda: Yeah? You're still not divulging everything that you know?

Jesse: No. I can't. ***For the sake of my country***. Listen, I was a trained intelligence officer. Once you do that, it's with you for life. I wish we had "Intelligence" today like we had then. We don't have an Intelligence [Department] today in this country. You know why? The news media took over everything. And politicians!

Linda: Well, that's what I feel is going to try to get through and break through [secrets] ... the news media ... and maybe through this book [*The Roswell Incident*].

Jesse: Maybe so. I don't know.

Linda: Because you can't keep it [UFO secrets] from today's press.

Jesse: Now, those guys, Charles Berlitz and William Moore, I bet I have spent as much as ten hours along these telephones with these two guys. I've never met either one of them.

Linda: Really? Just over the phone, huh?

Jesse: I have never met them. They interviewed me on the phone.

Linda: On the phone. And you sent them those pictures? They got the pictures that's in there [*The Roswell Incident* book]?

Jesse: Yeah. They went to Roswell, New Mexico and got that [photo of Jesse squatting down near debris]. (See Figure 1)

Linda: How old are you in that picture?

Jesse: I was 40 years old.

Linda: You look younger than 40 in there [photo]. I swear, I thought you were about late 20s.

Jesse: Well, I was happy. You see, I flew a lot of combat. I loved that life.

Linda Corley, Ph.D.

Major Jesse Marcel in 1947

Figure 1

Linda: And this is what? Like that foil that they described in here [*The Roswell Incident* book].

Jesse: What you see there is nothing but a piece of brown paper that I put over so that the news media couldn't get a picture of what I had. [Referring to the above photo found on page 34 of *The Roswell Incident* book]

Linda: Oh, you were covering the stuff?

Jesse: I was covering it, yeah. But nobody knew that. I was told by my commanding General, "Just don't say anything. Don't show anything." And the moment he walked into that room, I had a long pow-pow with him in his office.

Linda: Good looking, huh? [Asked of Mrs. Marcel about photo of Jesse]

Jesse: [I am] all eyes.

Mrs. Marcel: Oh, he looked like he was from Mars to me. (Laughter)

Linda: He looks a lot younger [than 40].

COVER UP BY AIR FORCE

Jesse: You see this picture right here? *[Photo of General Ramey on page 35 of The Roswell Incident]* That's a fake. After I left there ... he's the Commanding General ... General Ramey. He claimed that it was fragments of a weather balloon. So they took this [photo]. This is part of a weather balloon. They had that picture made here with this. I wasn't even there then. They had this picture made, strictly for the press.

Figure 2
General Ramey and Colonel DuBose

Linda: Yeah? But when they let the press take this picture [Marcel photo] they still told you to cover the stuff up?

Jesse: Right. Well, he didn't have to tell me that. I knew that.

Linda: Oh? You knew better than to show [debris]?

Jesse: That's what I did.

Linda: But didn't they think that people weren't going to be stupid enough to believe that it was a weather balloon like that? [Pointing to photo of weather balloon]

Jesse: I knew it wasn't a weather balloon. And General Ramey knew it wasn't a weather balloon. I want to show you something else. [Jesse left the room]

BERMUDA TRIANGLE MYSTERY

Jesse: *[When he returned]* You see this fellow right here? *[Pointing to photo on page 46 in The Roswell Incident]* That's Payne Jennings.

Figure 3
Lt. Col. Payne Jennings

I was scheduled for a flight to Europe, non-stop, with him. Now I don't know whether I'd be a co-pilot, navigator, or what. [Here again, speaking in the present time.] It was just a ... it was just ... we had the B-29 just fully loaded with gasoline. And I was scheduled to fly with him to Europe. Our first landing would be at Le Bourget Air Dome in France, in Paris. That morning, we were supposed to take off at ten. But at nine o'clock he called. [Pointing to photo on page 46 of *The Roswell Incident*]

Figure 4
Colonel Blanchard

He was my Commanding Officer, Col. Blanchard. He's from Boston. He's demised now, to my dismay. He was one of the finest Commanding Officers I've ever worked with. Well, anyway, I was supposed to take off with him. I had everything packed just ready to go. When he called me on the telephone and said, "Jesse." He said, "Just stay here." I said, "Yes sir." I said, "Why?" He said, "You have a V.I.P. that you have to entertain." And that was Col. Charles Lindbergh that was coming over.

Linda: Oh? And did you get to meet him?

Mrs. Marcel: I finally got to meet him at the Officer's Club.

Jesse: Yeah. We went to the Officer's Club and I had to feed him.

Linda: You had to feed him? (Laughter)

Mrs. Marcel: I'm glad it wasn't me.

Linda: Lindbergh himself. Oh, that must have been an honor, huh?

Jesse: And I told him that I was scheduled to fly to Le Bourget. He said, "That was the place I landed in *The Spirit of St. Louis*."

Linda: Say that name again?

Jesse: Le Bourget. It's French. I think it's <u>Toll</u> or something Air Drop now, just outside of Paris.

Linda: OK.

Jesse: That's where Lindbergh landed. And I was supposed to land there. And here the very man who landed *The Spirit of St. Louis* there. And I had him with me.

Linda: That's ironic, huh?

Jesse: OK. What happened then ... this is a mystery. Col. Payne Jennings and ... they've got another guy who was flying co-pilot for them ... either co-pilot or navigator, it could be either one. And they took off and once they crossed the east coast of Florida they were never heard from. They went into *The Bermuda Triangle*.

Linda: The Bermuda Triangle?

Jesse: The Bermuda Triangle. They were never heard from. Now, I would have been on that plane. Had it not been for Col. Lindbergh coming over. She [wife] knows that story. Boy!

Linda: Strange events, huh, around it? Gosh. Well, good. You're telling me stuff that's not in the book. [Referring to *The Roswell Incident*]

Jesse: Oh, that's right. I've got a hell of a lot I could tell you that's not in the book.

Linda: Oh, come on, tell me some more.

Mrs. Marcel: You ought to hear of the narrow escapes he's had. It's amazing. It makes you believe in fate, really.

[Here is more validation given to Jesse by Mrs. Marcel.]

Linda: It's almost like you're being taken care of. [Pointing to the sky]

Mrs. Marcel: Well, somebody up there must like him.

Linda: Somebody?

Jesse: Or maybe they don't want me.

Linda: Oh, I don't know. I don't think it's that.

Mrs. Marcel: Maybe they **don't** want you.

Linda: I would have never thought of it that way.

FLYING COMBAT

Jesse: I'll tell you something. I was flying combat one day. I got shot down. And the Japanese shot out three engines out of the B-24 we were flying in. I had to bail out. I had a back pack but on the way out of the plane ... I knew I had to go out. I couldn't stay in the plane. On the way out I picked up a little test pack and I put it on my parachute and I went out. I bailed out and I started

Linda Corley, Ph.D.

tumbling. I pulled the rip cord out of the doggone thing and that back pack never opened. I had bailed out from 8,000 feet. My back pack never opened. And I couldn't open it. You see, you have to reach back there to open it. So I went to my little test pack. I finally broke it with my finger. I broke that canvas and then I saw a piece of wire, of course I was tumbling, you see. And I saw a piece of wire starting to ease out. I thought it ... hit me like that. I was about 2,000 feet above the ground when it opened.

Linda: That makes you think, huh?

Mrs. Marcel: Well, he was picked up by the ...

Jesse: I was picked up by the natives and they quickly built a basket out of <u>kunir</u> grass ... was the same thing but they called it <u>pipe</u> ... but it looked mossy. They built the basket all right and they put me in there and they carried me in the stream and I realized I only had one shoe on. I had left a shoe in the ground.

Linda: In the ground? You had gone in the ground?

Jesse: Up to my knees.

Linda: Where was this at?

Jesse: In New Guinea.

Linda: In New Guinea?

Jesse: I said, "What the hell was a shoe anyway."

Linda: You got your legs and your feet, thank God.

Mrs. Marcel: And they weren't Japanese, so ...

Jesse: I saw this Sgt. _____ there and he ... When I got to the other side of the stream they had one of these little outriggers. They paddled me further upstream and decided where to pick me up. We went back to _____ then back to Fort Myers where I spent the night in the hospital. And I wasn't hurt except sore and the next morning ... that happened Christmas Eve, I spent Christmas day in the hospital and part of Christmas night. I went back to my outfit and my C.O. had me back in an airplane flying combat on the 26th of December.

Linda: Oh, goodness. What year was that?

Jesse: That was 1944. I mean '43.

Mrs. Marcel: You don't want to hear all that. You're straying from the book. [Referring to *The Roswell Incident*.]

Linda: I know, but it's so interesting to hear all that. Getting back to the book. OK. But you tell me anything you want to tell me. OK? This Brazel, is that how you say his name? Did you ever meet him?

Jesse: I had never met him before. I met him the day he came to Roswell with us.

Linda: Yeah, but you met him when the incident happened?

Jesse: Oh, yeah. In fact, I went to his house. I followed him. We left Roswell early in the afternoon and got there at dusk when we got there so we couldn't do anything that evening. So we stayed at his house that night with Cavitt [Sheridan]. He was a civilian but he was a ... he belonged to a forerunner of the CIA. I had three of those in my outfit working with me. All we did was run investigation. I had three of those guys with me. I took him and he and I went out there and spent the night at his house. We were treated with a can of pork and beans and crackers.

Linda: Isn't that something?

Jesse: And the next morning we got up and had to start picking up all this junk. We were at it all day long.

Linda: It was a lot, huh?

Jesse: Oh, Lord! It was about maybe a mile long and several hundred feet wide of debris.

Linda: This is the picture? *[Pointing to a photo of land in The Roswell Incident book on page 93]*

Jesse: This is approximately where it was but that is not a real picture. This whole thing is fake.

Linda: You mean the book or the picture? I was going to ask you what your opinion of the book was.

Jesse: The book is good. The picture is a fake. They went out there and took a picture of a random ... picture of flat land.

Linda: Of where they thought it might be?

Jesse: You see, there's flat land ...

Linda: All over the place.

Jesse: There's eighty square miles of flat land that all looks alike.

Mrs. Marcel: But you did find [location] ...

[More validation for Jesse from Mrs. Marcel]

Jesse: I did find ... the last time I was over there. We looked all day long for that place and I finally found it [in 1981].

Linda: After all those years.

Jesse: Yeah.

Linda: Yeah. They ought to mark it. I mean, if they're going to keep doing reports on it, they ought to mark it with something. Put a stake or something, you know? If they're going to keep...

For The Sake of My Country

[Little did I know then that it would indeed be marked one day. We had no way of knowing how big Roswell would become. Now, even boasting it's own UFO museum.]

Jesse: Well, the man who operates the ranch now is no longer the man ... is no longer Brazel. It's a man by the name of Bogle. Now the house that Brazel lived in is no longer visible. They built another house on top of it. This guy was very cooperative, to talk to him. Of course the whole landscape is no longer the same.

Linda: No? I guess not, after all those years.

HIEROGLYPHIC DRAWING

Linda: You know what interested me most about the whole thing was the writings that ... they say in the book ... were on the wood or the Hieroglyphic pictures or whatever. That, I find, was fascinating.

Jesse: That is something that we never deciphered what it was. There's a lot of it. I brought some stuff to her [wife]. My wife saw that.

Linda: Was it drawings or what?

Mrs. Marcel: I was the first one to say that it was Hieroglyphics of some sort.

Linda: You were the first to say that, huh?

Mrs. Marcel: Yeah. But I wouldn't know what it was.

Jesse: They tried to decipher that stuff. But as far as I know, they never did.

Linda: The book said something about it didn't have drawings of animals, other than that, it looked like Hieroglyphs?

Linda Corley, Ph.D.

Mrs. Marcel: Yeah. It looked like some kind of symbols. I should have said symbols instead of Hieroglyphics.

Linda: Yeah. It is symbols. Not all Hieroglyphs have the animals. I studied that on my own for awhile and I can write ... I have some painting I've done and some writings I've done in Hieroglyphs and not all of them have animals. *[Referring to Demotic Hieroglyphs - See Figure 9]*

Mrs. Marcel: I said, "Hey, that's Hieroglyphics!"

Linda: You can still see that in your mind. I wish you could draw it. You think you could draw it?

Jesse: Oh, Lord!

Mrs. Marcel: Little Jesse tried to draw it. [Referring to her son]

Jesse: Jesse tried to draw ... it was so irregular ... I mean ...

[He meant that the symbols were irregular, not the beams.]

Linda: Why don't you try it?

Mrs. Marcel: There wasn't anything to it. Let me see if I can find it.

[She searched the kitchen for son's drawing.]

Jesse: Maybe she can probably ...

Linda: Yeah. But you saw it a lot. Just give me an example. That would be fantastic!

[I could hardly hold in my excitement at the prospect of Jesse actually drawing the craft beam and writings that he held in his hands and had in his house in 1947.]

Mrs. Marcel: Let me see if it's still in here. [She continued to look for son's drawing.]

Jesse: No, no. Jesse [junior] didn't have that right, to begin with. [Referring to son's drawing]

Mrs. Marcel: Well, OK. You draw it then.

Jesse: He [junior] said they looked like "I" beams. But it wasn't.

Mrs. Marcel: Cause I wasn't really interested. I just wanted it out of my house.

Jesse: There were figures like this ... others like this ... others like that ... others like that ... curves ... this way ... that way. [He drew a rough sketch of symbols.]

Linda: All going from left to right like ...? [Referring to the symbols]

Jesse: Well, you can't tell.

Linda: Was it a beam?

Jesse: It was on a beam. It was about ... most of it ... Let me give you a cross section of what it looked like. About this wide ... about this thick ... like this. It looked like that. Beams were approximately that size. Some a little larger, some a little smaller. They ranged anywhere from four or five inches long to three or four feet long.

[He drew a sketch of a beam. One end of the beam was closed and the other was open. This could be due to several factors such as the possibility that he did not want to complete the beam, or that he felt he could not draw well enough to complete the beam, or the beam was broken off at one end. We will never know.]

Linda Corley, Ph.D.

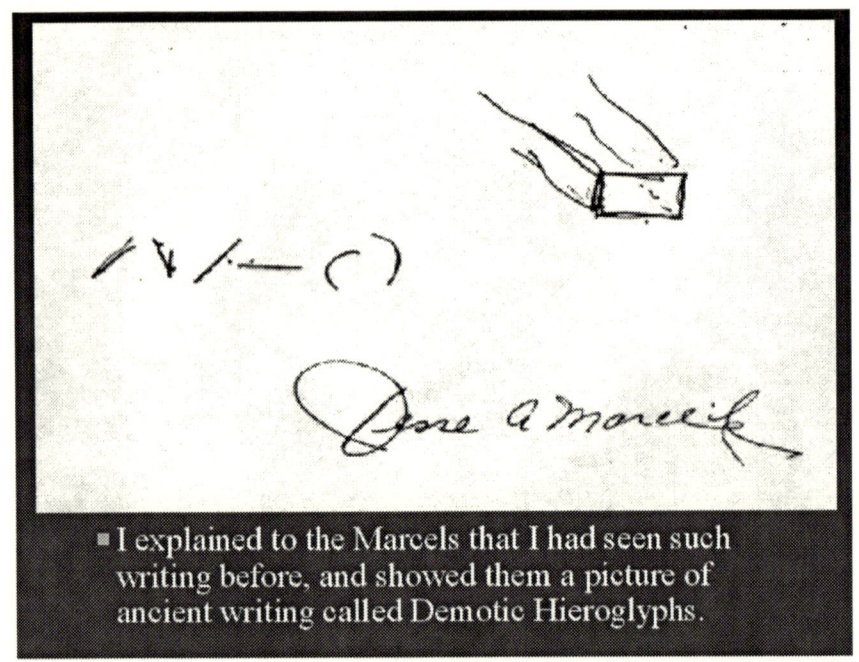

> ■ I explained to the Marcels that I had seen such writing before, and showed them a picture of ancient writing called Demotic Hieroglyphs.

Figure 5
Jesse's Signed Drawing

Linda: Now this is the wood stuff ... that looked like wood?

Jesse: What appeared to be wood. And this right here... along it [beam]. [Pointing to the symbols]

[What appeared to be wood to me and what appeared to be wood to Jesse could be two different things. However, having seen the same kinds of wood we see every day in this area of the country, I felt that we had the same or similar images of wood in our minds at this time. If there would have been a need for Jesse to explain that the wood did not look like any wood from this area but resembled wood from another country, I feel that he would have discussed this with me in order to help me get a picture in my mind of what he saw.]

Linda: Now I've got a good picture of it in my mind.

Jesse: I hope you have a good mind. (Laughter)

Linda: You said something about it [symbols] being colored ... or colors?

Jesse: Yeah. They were purple and pink. Kind of a ... the main character might be pink and the tone behind it was purple. The others were purple ... and switched around. But it didn't mean anything. [See Figures 12, 13, & 14]

Linda: But you could tell it was supposed to mean something?

Jesse: It was supposed to mean something.

Linda: It's not just decoration?

Jesse: It could have been. It could have been ... something for assembling the thing. I don't know. This is a conjecture. What is conjecture? It's an opinion that you can't verify as fact.

Linda: Yeah. But it's a fair opinion because it's yours and you saw it and you handled it. So that raised the opinion a little more in favor of credibility.

Jesse: What they're trying to make me say, "Do you really know that it came from outer space?" I don't. How can I say that? All I know is the material that I found and carried to the base ... The only thing I can say is that it might indicate that it might have been from out of space. It's nothing I had ever seen before. And I haven't seen it since. Even modern manufacturing and processes that we have now ... all the materials they have ... I've never seen anything like that.

Linda: The foil that you said ... if you wrinkle it and lay it down it gets its shape again?

Jesse: Well, you couldn't wrinkle it. You see this foil? *[Pointed to a cigarette package on the table]* You know the thickness of that? That's thin. I found a piece about this wide and about this long. About two feet long. And I had a very genius fellow working for me in my office. See, way back then, I was so busy running a business.

Linda Corley, Ph.D.

See, after all, I had twenty clerk-typists, plus five officers working for me. Plus three counter-intelligence agents. I had to keep up with what they were doing. He said, "I saw something unusual." I said, "What's that?" He said, "You see this piece of metal?" He said, "I tried to bend it, tried to make a mark on it. You can't make a mark on it." I said, "Come on, you're kidding me." So I went out there. He took a sixteen pound sledgehammer and put the piece of metal on the ground and he hit it like that and it bounced off it.

Linda: So you couldn't fold it, bend it, wrinkle it, or nothing?

Jesse: You couldn't even dent it with a sledgehammer. Thin as this. *[Pointing to the cigarette pack]* And when you had it in your hand you had nothing. It was as light as balsa wood.

Linda: And it wouldn't burn, I think you said?

Jesse: Nope. You couldn't make a mark on that stuff. Like these little members there. [Pointing to the drawing of the beam] I took my cigarette lighter and tried to burn some of that. It wouldn't burn. What appeared to be wood. It wasn't wood.

Linda: It wasn't wood.

Jesse: Uh uh. But what was it? I still don't know.

Linda: So you have something that looks like tin, something that looks like wood. Is there anything else? There was something about string mentioned ... twine or silk?

Jesse: That, I didn't see myself. See, many other people went out there.

CHAPTER TWO
A PERSONAL THEORY OF UFOs

> I think the method of propulsion moves to the fourth dimension. I think when they have the ability to change from the third dimension to the fourth dimension - there is no time. They can be here one second and the next second they could be millions and millions of miles away ... light years away.
>
> ~~ JESSE A. MARCEL, SR.

EXTRATERRESTRIAL TEACHERS

Linda: I don't feel that they're here to hurt anybody. I've always believed in them. And I feel that they could ...

Mrs. Marcel: Well, I think they're probably trying to teach us something.

Linda: I do too. That's a popular opinion, what you're saying. A lot of people feel that way. Because by now, with their technology, they could have killed us. I mean, you have to trust them. And there is something in the book [*The Roswell Incident*] that really was pretty. It said, "It's as hard to deny now as it's going to be not to deny in the future." Or something like that.

Jesse: That was written by Charles Berlitz. Well, he's a good writer.

Linda Corley, Ph.D.

Linda: "It's as impossible to confirm them in the present as it will be to deny them in the future." [Reading the quote from the book] I've never heard it put so well. Do you think the book [*The Roswell Incident*] was really accurate?

Jesse: Yes. It's very accurate. They went into detail in everything I discussed with them.

[*How did he know this if he had not read the book?*]

Linda: OK. There is a C.A.U.S. - Citizens Against UFO Secrecy. That organization said that they went to court in CAUS vs. US Air Force, to get the records?

Jesse: I heard about that but I don't know.

Linda: They named a Col. John Bowen, in charge. But you were the first one sent out. And they said they wanted to summons the records plus this man. But who is John Bowen?

Jesse: I never heard of him.

Linda: That's in the book.

Jesse: I read that, yeah.

[*Was this confirmation that he had indeed read the book?*]

Mrs. Marcel: I didn't read the book.

[*It appeared that neither one of the Marcels had any knowledge about the specific topics covered or not covered in the book. However, I felt that Jesse would know what I wanted in an "exclusive" and that being something he had not given to any other interviewer.*]

Linda: Yeah, Col. John Bowen. And the US Air Force was supposed to have gone to court in 1978 for those records. And I wondered why they didn't want to talk to you.

Jesse: They never contacted me.

Linda: You were the first one ...

Jesse: I was the very first one. I was the very first one to ever handle the stuff.

Mrs. Marcel: I know that. Oh brother, do I.

[Up to this point, Mrs. Marcel showed little interest in participating in the discussion. I was glad that she was beginning to feel more comfortable with me.]

Linda: If they would have called you into court, it might have been a whole different thing. Maybe now that the book is out, they will. I don't know.

Mrs. Marcel: When he left, he didn't tell me where he was going or anything. And all of a sudden, I was swarmed with reporters and I didn't know what it was all about.

Linda: You got out-foxed. You see what I mean about the press? The media is going to get something if they can.

Mrs. Marcel: But how they got it, I don't know. Cause he was still out there.

Jesse: Well, they got it from our Public Relations Officer.

Mrs. Marcel: Whoever. You mean Walter Haut?

Jesse: Yeah.

Linda: What about the teletype? This lady had sent this teletype?

Jesse: Well, to me that's hearsay. I don't know anything about it.

Linda: Yeah, you don't know for sure, huh? What was her name?

Jesse: [It was sent] between Roswell and Albuquerque.

Linda Corley, Ph.D.

Linda: I have it written down. What's her name? Lydia, Mrs. Lydia Sleppy. Teletype on July seventh.... told of the craft. [Reading from my notes] And she was told to forget what she had just heard. So the media ... the reporters could have gotten that from that?

Jesse: Well you see, Berlitz and Moore investigated this thing to the hilt.

Linda: Yes I know. I can tell.

Mrs. Marcel: Well, when you try to cover up something ...

Linda: Then you know there is something [to cover up] ... yeah.

ALIEN AUTOPSY

Linda: And he also, in the book, had something about ... There was an autopsy done on some of the bodies ... Dr. Weisberg?

Jesse: Yeah. I took that with a grain of salt. There is a character in Cincinnati, Ohio that spent a lot of time on the telephone with me. He said that he knew a doctor who performed an autopsy on one of the figures that was found. I said, "Well, I don't know anything about that."

Linda: No? You don't? But do you think that it's possible because now that you've stayed quiet all these years that other people are going to start talking too? Now that you ...

Jesse: Maybe so. I just don't know.

Linda: It's gotten to the point where it happened so long ago.

Jesse: Except that anybody they interview today wouldn't have had the responsibility that I had. My responsibility was to keep my mouth shut.

Linda: But I'm sure they all felt that way. Because everybody kept quiet.

Jesse: Right.

Mrs. Marcel: When they start finding bodies though, why don't they show them to somebody and let us see what they look like?

Linda: They think that we're going to panic. I really can't believe that the government thinks we're going to panic. You know, there's a paragraph in the book that satisfies me just a little bit about why ... why don't you want to tell us. And it says, "If any nation could figure out how those UFOs operated they could duplicate it and then they would be in control of the world."

Jesse: That's right.

Mrs. Marcel: That's the only thing?

Linda: And that's the only reason they don't want us to know?

Mrs. Marcel: Yeah. They might be trying to find out how this metal was made and everything.

Jesse: Maybe so. I had thought about that.

Linda: That won't stop them from controlling the world. How can we stop what the Air Force or the Government or anybody is doing just by knowing that it [alien craft] exists?

FOURTH DIMENSION

Jesse: All I can say is this. If maybe the Air Force is still working on trying to define the method of propulsion of those things. Cause the method of propulsion, after all, I've had quite a bit of Physics. I think the method of propulsion moves to the fourth dimension.

Linda Corley, Ph.D.

Linda: Yeah? Tell me more.

Jesse: Well, in the fourth dimension, there is no time. To give you an idea. I don't know how much Astronomy you know. I've studied quite a bit of Astronomy myself and how planets were formed. How a planet will go through a black hole and time no longer exists. It can be one way or the other. That's the fourth dimension. Once you go through one of those black holes.

[Throughout the interview, Jesse stated that he did not read. Not even the book about his experiences. However, in this statement he admits that he has studied extensively on the subjects of Physics and Astronomy, including the black hole theory which was not popular until the 1970s. I assumed that he was no longer reading on this subject matter as he was no longer interested in it. But now I was also convinced that at one time, after 1947, he was an avid reader on the subject of UFOs, space travel, physics, and astronomy.]

Linda: But what does that have to do with the levitating device and the propulsion and the fuel it uses or whatever?

Jesse: Well, do they use any fuel? We don't know.

Linda: But how would the time affect that?

Jesse: I think when they have the ability to change from the third dimension to the fourth dimension, there is no time. They can be here one second and the next second they could be millions and millions of miles away... light years away.

Mrs. Marcel: Like Buck Rogers' 25th Century, huh?

Jesse: Yeah.

Linda: Well, you know how all of the science fiction has come true so far?

Mrs. Marcel: I believe in keeping an open mind.

For The Sake of My Country

Linda: Oh yeah. You can't be that narrow minded to believe we're the only people. I mean, that's too narrow minded.

Jesse: Good God! When you realize that Earth is the youngest planet in our Galaxy.

Mrs. Marcel: And how big and how old it is.

Linda: And all of the other galaxies that we don't even know of, that we're just finding.

Jesse: Right.

Linda: Oh, what's your opinion... I'm going to throw this in quick. What's your opinion of the... have you read *The Interrupted Journey*?" Betty and Barney Hill?

Jesse: No, no.

Mrs. Marcel: I read that.

Jesse: She reads a lot. I don't read.

[Here he clearly states that he does not read.]

Linda: Yeah, but you would enjoy it.

Mrs. Marcel: That [book] was good.

Linda: And the movie *Close Encounters*, the little aliens they made for that movie, it's amazing.

Mrs. Marcel: Oh, brother! I felt like running when I say that movie.

Linda: Did you enjoy the movie?

Mrs. Marcel: Oh, I enjoyed it.

Linda Corley, Ph.D.

Jesse: I understand those things and I think I understand a whole lot more than I can talk about on this subject. Sometimes, you keep on talking that way ... people will get a net after you.

[This statement appears to insinuate that he had some knowledge still not yet divulged concerning UFOs and Beings from another planet.]

Linda: I don't believe so much today ... that anymore. They used to. I used to not be able to talk about [paranormal] things like that. Now, you can go to school and get degrees in it. So I mean ... you've got to feel free to have an open mind and speak your mind. People have been quiet too many years about this. That's why everybody's ignorant about it.

Jesse: I fully share that with you.

THIRTY TWO YEAR SILENCE

Jesse: But this whole theory in this book [*The Roswell Incident*] right there. For thirty two years I held out. I didn't talk to anybody. And Stanton Friedman came to LSU and gave a lecture on Nuclear Physics and flying saucers. There's a guy in Baton Rouge. He's retired now. He told Stanton Friedman, he said, "The guy you ought to talk to is Jesse Marcel in Houma." Cause he remembered reading about me in 1947 when all that came out. And of course, it was scrubbed. See, back then ... So Stanton Friedman called me. He was at Tulane. He gave a lecture at Tulane [University]. And he called me from New Orleans. Well, to make a long story short, Stanton Friedman sat on my front porch out there with a filming crew out from Los Angeles and we went through the whole story.

Mrs. Marcel: Boy, it was 92 degrees outside and about 110 degrees in the patio.

Jesse: They had me sitting on a chair out there. It was 92 degrees outside, there were hot lights.

Linda: When was that?

Jesse: It was 1979. In May 1979.

Linda: Well, what are they doing with this film? I want to see it.

Jesse: They were filming a documentary on flying saucers.

Linda: I'd like to see it when it comes on TV.

Mrs. Marcel: It's never shown here.

Jesse: It's never been shown here. They filmed me right there [pointing to patio] for six hours. I sweated blood for six hours out there.

Linda: Oh, I want to see that film.

Mrs. Marcel: I sat in here with the air conditioner on and laughed at him.

Linda: Why didn't they come in?

Mrs. Marcel: I don't know. They wanted the patio in the background.

Linda: I'll bet it's pretty. I bet it filmed good.

Mrs. Marcel: Oh, it's terrible. Every once in a while the roof would beat against ... it was a windy day and they had to stop filming.

Jesse: I don't know if it will be shown. I got a lot of letters from Stanton Friedman about the film. They had to cut out a whole lot of stuff that they filmed. That director ...

Linda Corley, Ph.D.

HOLLYWOOD MOVIE OFFER

Jesse: I'll tell you one thing. I got an offer right now. I could be in a Hollywood movie.

Linda: Are you gonna go?

Jesse: Hell no! I'm too old, Linda.

Mrs. Marcel: If he'd be 20 years younger.

Linda: Yeah, but you couldn't do it then. You would have responsibilities. You would have family. You would have work. Now, you can go.

Jesse: I got a job offer. There is no date.

Linda: You should take it. How many people can do that?

Jesse: I have one child. He's a medical doctor.

Linda: I know. Aren't you proud?

Jesse: Oh, I'm proud of him.

Mrs. Marcel: I hope they do show what he said. Boy, they spent an hour at least, on little Jesse. I hope they show it. He's trying to record it as it comes on the air.

Jesse: You know what they want me for right now?

Linda: What?

Jesse: To play with Archie Bunker.

Linda: In a scene about a UFO or just to play ...?

Jesse: No, no. On his show. Carroll O'Connor ... See I met him. I know him personally.

Linda: Oh, really?

Jesse: It's continuous filming. About ten hours a day. They offered me $10,000 a week for it.

Mrs. Marcel: I told him, "Go ahead, I'll stay and take care of the place. You go."

Jesse: Linda, after all, this month [May] I'll be 74 years old.

[He died in 1986 at age 79.]

Linda: I know. I was going to tell you Happy Birthday. I knew your birth date but …

Jesse: I'm retired and sometimes I think I'm retarded. (Laughter)

[Jesse had a great sense of humor and never appeared to take himself too seriously.]

Linda: It must be good just to stay home. But Hollywood? Come on. Not everybody gets asked to go to Hollywood.

Jesse: I'd feel like a doggone bee living in a bee hive out there.

Mrs. Marcel: Well, they bother you here.

Linda: Yeah. You're getting bothered here. Look at me. I'm bothering you today. (Laughter)

Jesse: No.

Mrs. Marcel: I don't feel like living in a bee hive.

Linda: But you wouldn't be living over there? You would just be going for that one thing.

Jesse: Oh, I need to sign a contract. At least a one or two year contract with them. Spending seven to fourteen hours a day on a film set. You know Archie Bunker's side kick named Murry? He's

Linda Corley, Ph.D.

quitting. I think Carroll O'Connor probably wants me to replace Murry.

Linda: Oh, you would be perfect in that [role]. Ya'll both behind the bar. I can see ya'll now. (Laughter)

Mrs. Marcel: Oh, I'm afraid he'd drink up all the profits. (Laughter)

Linda: You'd have a good time.

Jesse: I just can't make up my mind to do that.

Linda: Sometimes you're not asked until it's just the right time. And now might be just the right time. You would have the qualities that they need for that particular thing now, not when you were younger.

Jesse: Carroll O'Connor knows me personally. I met him and had a long talk with him. You would never know that he was a University college professor who taught English.

Linda: Do you know any other movie stars?

Jesse: Oh, yeah. Do you know Burgess Merideth? He was my student at the Air Intelligence School. You know Gene Raymond? You've heard of him? He hung around with Jeanette McDonald. He was in our class at the Intelligence School. I've mingled with a lot of movie personalities.

Linda: Ever met any Presidents?

Jesse: This is the best I did ... I had dinner with the Vice President of the United States.

Mrs. Marcel: The one they call the V. I. P.?

Jesse: That was Wallace. I sat with him and had dinner at _____ __. They were instructors at the Air Academy.

Linda: How long did you stay in Roswell?

Jesse: In Roswell? I was there from ... let's see ... I came back from overseas in 1945. I was there from 1945 to 1948.

Linda: Then where were you sent after Roswell?

Jesse: To Washington. They [military] give you a calendar about this long [gesturing] and a secretary. I didn't know what my duties were going to be.

Linda: Well, why do you think they did that? *[Referring to the transfer to Washington]*

Jesse: They wanted to get me out of Roswell and get me out of there. But first of all it had been requested that I be sent to the Air Intelligence School as an instructor. My Commanding Officer, Col. Blanchard put his foot down and said, "He's too valuable here." By telling you this, you seem bored.

[I'm not sure what kind of look I had on my face at this time, but Jesse took it to mean boredom. Believe me, it was not boredom. My mind was always racing ahead to think of the next question that I would ask him. A question that I felt he would be willing to answer. I was a bit cautious about asking anything that might be too embarrassing.]

Linda: No. You've got something to be proud of. You talk about it.

Jesse: But I'm telling you the truth. Well, anyway, when Col. Blanchard refused to transfer me to Air Intelligence School as an instructor, three months later a direct order came out of Washington that I had to go to headquarters ... to the Strategic Air Command at Andrews Air Force Base. And when I got there I didn't know what I was going to do. They gave me a secretary.

[In retelling of this experience, Jesse still seemed to wonder about the motives of his superiors. His repeated statements about being given

Linda Corley, Ph.D.

a secretary, as simple as it may sound, didn't make much sense to him then.]

PROMOTION TO LT. COL.

Linda: When did they make you a Lt. Colonel?

Jesse: In 1948.

Linda: Oh, really?

Jesse: You want a little more ice in that?

[He was referring to my glass of wine. About this time, we were settling in to a very comfortable conversational pattern. We had several glasses of wine during this interview and it made for a relaxed and laid back atmosphere which contributed to the various topics and easy flow of conversation about personal matters that Jesse and his wife shared with me, a complete stranger to them.]

Linda: Thank you.

Jesse: I've got a little story to tell you about that. When my promotion came through, I was in …

Mrs. Marcel: He didn't even know he was promoted.

Jesse: My secretary filed my papers and that file was no longer in my personal file. That got lost. I didn't lose my personnel file. The military did. I didn't know I was a Lt. Col. till I got out of the service.

[This statement leads me to believe that a certain portion of Jesse's military record no longer existed.]

Linda: Oh, no.

Jesse: That's right.

Mrs. Marcel: You looked through ... the other day you were looking through your files ...

[Could "the other day" have meant two years ago? In previous interviews given by Jesse in the last two years, it was indicated that he was a Lt. Col.]

Linda: Just till the other day? Thirty years have passed and you didn't know?

Mrs. Marcel: He was looking through his files and said, "Heck, I'm a Lt. Col. and didn't know it."

Linda: Are you kidding?

Mrs. Marcel: No he's not kidding.

Jesse: I made Lt. Col. in December 1948. I got out of the service in 1950.

Linda: And all these years ....?

[I was having a good deal of trouble grasping the fact that so many years had gone by before he discovered that he was promoted to Lt. Col. I felt that I was missing something here but I did not know what.]

Mrs. Marcel: He was going through the files looking up stuff on this [Roswell and UFOs].

Linda: Can you believe [that]? In '48 you were a Lt. Col. and didn't even know it.

Jesse: Didn't even know it.

Linda: Till this year ... '81?

Jesse: Yeah.

Linda Corley, Ph.D.

[He may not have realized that this information was in "The Roswell Incident" which he gave an interview for in 1979, two years prior to this meeting.]

Linda: This is beautiful. I love it. That's a good story. All that time. (Laughter)

Mrs. Marcel: All that time.

Jesse: Linda, I went through a hell of a lot in my life. I mean I was an ambitious guy. You might have heard the expression "Cat on a tin roof?"

Linda: A cat on a hot tin roof?

Jesse: I was like ten cats on a hot tin roof. Don't touch me.

Linda: Well, did you hear anything more after you got to Washington? About anything? Nothing ever again, huh?

Jesse: No.

Linda: Until '79? Until 1979? Nothing from Washington till '79?

[I was trying to point out the year that was mentioned in "The Roswell Incident" book. His promotion was mentioned in 1979. I still felt that we were not communicating clearly on this fact.]

Jesse: See, the personnel department never picked that up.

[He was trying to give me more clarity on this subject as I was making it known to him that I was still confused about the matter.]

Linda: They didn't, huh?

Jesse: So I just don't know what to say about that.

[Giving up on this subject was all he could do at this time. He had said all that he knew about it. Or had he?]

Linda: You see that look he gets in his eyes when he knows he's not going to tell me something. When he says, "No, I'm not going to tell you that!"

Mrs. Marcel: Unless he's telling you a fib.

[I don't' know why Mrs. Marcel insinuated that Jesse was lying about his promotion, when she was in fact the first one to bring up the subject that this indeed was the case.]

Jesse: This is not a fib! This is not a fib I'm telling you.

[Jesse then got up from the table and left the kitchen. While he was gone, I took this opportunity to inquire of Mrs. Marcel whether or not she thought Jesse was still keeping some Roswell events a secret.]

Mrs. Marcel: You can try to figure him out but I haven't.

Linda: Do you think you know everything that he isn't supposed to tell?

Mrs. Marcel: No!

Linda: You don't even know?

Mrs. Marcel: No.

Linda: How can anybody keep something inside like that?

Mrs. Marcel: I don't believe half he's saying. (Laughter)

[There are several statements made throughout the interview suggesting the possibility of a "fib" or a "lie" being told to me by Jesse. Were these lies about Roswell, the military, or his personal life, I don't know. Mrs. Marcel might have known for a fact that some things were indeed lies or possibly the closer to the truth we got the more implications of lies were suggested.]

Linda: Do you feel that he's still keeping a secret like he was told to? Still keeping quiet?

Linda Corley, Ph.D.

Mrs. Marcel: I don't' know.

[She could have answered an emphatic no to this question. If she really wanted to end this discussion and settle my mind on the subject, she could have answered no. Her answer only made me wonder what else Jesse was not telling.]

Linda: He made a remark a while ago about … There's a lot he's still not telling cause he was told not to. You know … and that all [information] in the book is a lot … but it's still not everything.

Mrs. Marcel: I don't know. I can't figure him out and I've been married to him for … How many years?

Linda: Can you imagine? After all that time? And still…

Mrs. Marcel: Forty five [years] … yeah … and still don't know him.

Linda: That's a long time. At least he's an interesting personality. When you can't know somebody, even though you live with them all those years and you really still can't know them.

Mrs. Marcel: Well, it makes for an interesting life.

[Jesse returned to the table]

COMMENDATION FROM NAVY

Jesse: There's my promotion.

[He handed me a piece of paper.]

Linda: Oh, look. Antoine.

[Reading from the paper, I noticed his middle name was the same as my grandfather.]

Jesse: This is one thing that I'm most proud of right here.

Linda: Lt. Col. Air Corp. [Reading from the paper] Oh, let me see.

[Here was a paper with his promotion of Lt. Col. clearly indicated.]

Jesse: It's a commendation from the United States Navy.

Linda: The Navy? How did you get a commendation from the Navy? Oh dear, are you going to tell me ...

Jesse: I won't tell you if you read it.

Linda: All right, OK. ***"Joint Task Force One. The Commander of Joint Task Force One takes pleasure in commending Major Jesse A. Marcel, Army of the United States, for services as set forth in the following citation. For superior performance of duty as Intelligence Officer of the 509th Composite Group and the Air Attack Unit 1.5.1 Joint Task Force One during the period from February to 16th of August 1946. With faithfully assigned personnel you built your entire program to the superior status that it achieved. It was through your previous knowledge that you were able to train your personnel to perform the many and varied duties and further to assemble the vast amount of information required in the training of the crews for their part in the Atomic Bomb test. You were not allowed to concentrate on the one paramount objective but were required also to promulgate an overall security plan and supervise the population both at the home base and on Kwajalein Island."***

Jesse: Kwajalein, off Bikini.

Linda: Kwajalein Island, OK. ***"To your devotion to duty you materially aided the advancement of Operation Cross Roads and the successful conduct of the Atomic Bomb Test. W.H.P. Blandy - Admiral U.S. Navy."***

Jesse: Correct.

Linda Corley, Ph.D.

Linda: Operation Cross Roads. That was the name of it, huh?

Jesse: That's right.

Linda: Wow!

Jesse: I had it under my wing. I guarantee. I had the responsibility of the whole thing. Army Intelligence was ready to transmit from one department to another.

Linda: This [document] is nice. You should frame it.

Jesse: Well, this is the one I'm proud of.

Linda: Ramey?

Jesse: Yeah. Ramey, he's the guy who was Commanding General of the 8th Air Force. He's the guy that I brought all that debris to. He's dead now.

Linda: You're not in contact with any of the people that were involved in that incident, huh?

Jesse: No.

Linda: None? And haven't been since you left Roswell?

Mrs. Marcel: I think they've all died.

Jesse: Well, a lot of those people contacted me but I don't have the ... I don't pursue all this stuff cause I'm no longer interested in this stuff. To be ... that's behind my back. I just don't ...

Linda: Yeah, but you had it for 32 years. We just got it in 1979.

Jesse: I know.

Linda: You've got to give us time to get used to that. Somebody who finally wants to talk [about UFOs].

For The Sake of My Country

DESTINATION OF DEBRIS

Linda: Did you see the movie *"Hanger 18"* that's supposed to be based on this?

[I felt that an indirect way to get to Jesse's feelings on UFOs was to present things that were not directly related to him. Therefore, he could feel safe in his discussion of the events, yet would reveal his thoughts on the issues.]

Jesse: No. I heard about it.

Mrs. Marcel: I saw it. It was good.

Linda: How do you feel about that? They say that it [UFO] was brought to Arlington ... wait ... I have it *[looking through my notes]* ... not Arlington, Virginia.

Jesse: Well, Arlington, Virginia ... there's an Air Base there. I took bombing instruction there. [I took] Navigation instruction there.

Mrs. Marcel: Oh, honey. Where did they bring it? You know where they brought it. It wasn't Arlington, it was ...

Jesse: They were supposed to bring the stuff at ...

Linda: Edwards Air Force Base and then chucked to California. Muroc, California? [Reading from my notes]

Jesse: Edwards Air Force Base is in California but the stuff that I gathered was supposed to have gone to Detroit.

Linda: Detroit?

[I wondered if Jesse was giving me an exclusive. Did he mean to say Dayton, Ohio? Or was it just poor memory on his part?]

Jesse: Yeah. I was supposed to fly it by myself.

Linda: And they pulled you from it, huh?

65

Jesse: General Ramey pulled me off it and said, "You stay right here. Go back to Roswell."

Linda: They sent someone who didn't know what was going on, probably.

Jesse: Well, he was the Commanding General.

Linda: Yeah, but they replaced you with somebody who probably didn't know what was going on.

Jesse: That's right. That's right.

Linda: They say that *Hanger 18* is in Wright-Patterson Air Force in Ohio.

Jesse: That's right.

Mrs. Marcel: Oh, that's where it was supposed to have been flown, wasn't it?

Jesse: Yeah.

Linda: And then the CIA compound in Langley, Virginia. It supposedly went there. And then McDill Air Force Base in Florida is where it's supposed to be ... where it's at now ... says the book [*The Roswell Incident*].

Jesse: Well, you see, that's ... a lot of this stuff ... I know nothing about.

Linda: You have no way of knowing?

Mrs. Marcel: Yeah, but Jesse told me over and over that it [debris] was flown to Wright-Patterson Air Force [Base].

Jesse: Yeah. I was supposed to fly it there myself.

[Here it becomes clear that it was not Detroit. Poor memory was probably the reason for the statement on Detroit.]

Linda: That was your mission and they scrubbed you from that?

Jesse: That was my mission. That was my order from my own Commanding Officer.

Linda: And you didn't ask any questions. The military professional you are, you didn't say nothing.

Jesse: No.

Linda: They trained him [well], huh? Boy they brainwash you when you're in the service.

Mrs. Marcel: Well, you're in the service, period!

Linda: That's right.

Jesse: You see, when they train you as an intelligence officer, you become an intelligence officer. And it lives with you the rest of your life. You're taught how to read. I could read pages upon pages of documents and burn it and recite it all over again.

Linda: And still know it?

Jesse: I could do that when I was younger. I couldn't do that now. But that's the clear mark of an intelligence officer. That's to stack it up there [pointing to head]. Forget about it.

Linda: Do you know if the house is still there, where you lived in Roswell?

Mrs. Marcel: He found it.

Jesse: Oh, yeah. I went in it.

Mrs. Marcel: Oh, the house we were living in is still there and been sold to a young couple and Jesse went back into it the other day and boy ...

[Here again a reference to "the other day" and in this instance was indeed a couple of years ago.]

Jesse: They showed me the whole thing. They've enlarged it.

Mrs. Marcel: They had the book [*The Roswell Incident*]. They wanted it autographed.

Jesse: You have no idea how many books I had to autograph for people.

Linda: If this wasn't a library book, I'd be asking for your autograph, too. You can autograph the Hieroglyphs. That's OK. (Laughter)

[Jesse signed his name under the drawing of the craft beam he had drawn for me earlier.]

Linda: Have they [young couple] been bothered, I wonder? No one knows that that is the house?

Jesse: No. It's a young couple who just bought the house. Honey, tell her how much we paid for the house.

Mrs. Marcel: Oh, I'd say $7,000 and they paid $48,000.

Linda: What about when you moved to Washington? You didn't like that, huh?

CHAPTER THREE
A CUMULATIVE EFFECT OF EVENTS

> Well, I've got what I want right here. We've got everything. I already have what I want. Why should I want more?
>
> ~ JESSE MARCEL, SR.

AIR FORCE CAREER

Jesse: She and I had a lot of experiences. I traveled from the time I got in the Air Force.

Linda: And when was that?

Jesse: I got in the Air Force in 1942.

Mrs. Marcel: 1941, huh?

Jesse: '41. I was commissioned in the Air Force in 1942. That's what it was.

Linda: OK. And you got out in ...?

Jesse: I got out in 1948 ... I mean '50. Well, I actually had eight and a half years of continuous active duty.

Linda: Why didn't you ... you didn't want to make it life?

Linda Corley, Ph.D.

Jesse: I got sick and tired of military life.

Mrs. Marcel: I got tired of moving my plants around.

Linda: Could you tell me something that is not in the book?

Jesse: I don't know what I could tell you that's not in the book. I haven't heard the whole book myself.

[This statement led me to believe that Jesse didn't read due to poor vision but had books read to him.]

Linda: No?

Mrs. Marcel: Well, you know, when you live something you don't have to read it.

Linda: O. K.

[As hard as I tried, I could not get Jesse to expand on his original story. However, he would try to accommodate my constant requests for "something not in the book" by telling me personal anecdotes that had little or nothing to do with the UFO incident itself but were just as interesting.]

Jesse: I can tell you something. Well, I was looking around these ranches out there.... now this happened in the middle of an 80 square mile ranch. Where this thing fell, right. I followed the whole thing out there. And it was dusk when we got there... so I didn't... You see, in New Mexico you don't have land marks. It's just wide open country. When I went back out there to look for it, I went to a place that I thought might be it. We stopped at a place and we ran into a lot of these illegal aliens in New Mexico. And once they see you coming boy they just clam up and close everything. They won't talk to you. I got to this place and we finally talk to this old boy. And they had a big Collie dog and I stepped out of the car and this Collie dog came to me. You see, a dog likes dogs. (Laughter) I started petting the dog. First thing I know, I looked around me there were about 25 goats around me.

Linda: (Laughter) Goats?

Mrs. Marcel: He's talking about this last visit.

Linda: Oh, this time?

Jesse: On this last visit, yeah. And I was petting the dog and the goats wanted to get petted, too. So I started petting the goats and I had a hard time keeping one or two of the goats from coming in the car with me.

Linda: Trained goats.

Jesse: I told Johnny Mann, who did the filming, you know. He said, "Good gosh." He says, "What are you doing with all the goats around here?" I said, "Well Johnny, when all the young goats like that see an old goat they want to meet him."

Linda: They want to know your secrets.

Jesse: Yeah, and I made him laugh.

Mrs. Marcel: Secrets of longevity I guess.

Linda: Well you sure have led an interesting life, I must say.

Jesse: Well, I'll have to agree with that; I have.

Linda: I still don't think it's over. I think you've got lots more you can do.

Mrs. Marcel: He could if he... he'd have to quit smoking first. His voice would get better.

Jesse: I've got emphysema.

Linda: I know.

[It was very hard for Jesse to speak clearly due to his emphysema.]

Linda Corley, Ph.D.

AUTOBIOGRAPHY PLANNED

Jesse: You know what I should do? And I've got what it takes to do it with. I ought to write an autobiography of my life.

Linda: Why don't you? That's a great idea.

Jesse: I've got a tape recorder. I've got about a dozen tapes. It would have to be typed so it could be assembled in the correct sequence.

Linda: You could have somebody to do all that. You just talk in the microphone and then you get the writers and they will do it because they will know that it's gonna sell.

Mrs. Marcel: Yeah, from the publicity of this book. (Referring to *The Roswell Incident* book)

Jesse: I could start from the time I was a kid in the country plowing an old white mule.

Linda: It would make a good book. That would give you something to do. I think I'd rather go to Hollywood, but if you don't want to go to Hollywood.

Jesse: I don't think I want to.

[This is in keeping with Jesse's statement about not wanting publicity. He never did go to Hollywood and he never did write that book.]

Linda: You don't want any attention like that?

Jesse: I don't. I don't... I don't like that. I feel that I'm a nobody and I'm going to keep on being a nobody.

Mrs. Marcel: Well, he's just run down cause he smokes too much.

Jesse: I know I'm run down. I don't take care of myself physically.

Mrs. Marcel: I used to smoke... but boy... I started getting a cough... I thought... blah! Let me tell you something. I quit cold turkey. That was really... it took me a year. Every time I'd see a cigarette lit on television, I'd want one.

ZODIAC SIGNS

Jesse: You're a Virgo?

Linda: No. I'm a Leo.

Jesse: I'm a Gemini.

Linda: Oh, need say no more! (Laughter)

Mrs. Marcel: You see what I mean? He's two people. They're interesting but hard to understand. I'm a Capricorn. I think they [Capricorns] can take a lot.

Linda: You look very calm. You look like you could cope with anything.

Mrs. Marcel: Well, I have to.

Linda: And you have.

Jesse: You know what gets me? I read the Astrographs in the paper. Virgos... anything about them pertains to financial things.

Mrs. Marcel: Little Jesse is a Virgo.

Jesse: Yeah, he's a Virgo.

Mrs. Marcel: Yeah, but I have to take high blood pressure pills but he doesn't. And I'm very calm.

Jesse: I don't know what I am.

Linda Corley, Ph.D.

Mrs. Marcel: I'm one person and that's it. I dreamed the other night I just threw dishes everywhere.

Linda: You're just suppressing all this anger you have and you've got to throw and break. (Laughter)

Mrs. Marcel: I sure did. Well, I'd do it if I didn't have to clean it up after.

Jesse: Well, I'll tell you. She can throw things... not necessarily in dreams. (Laughter)

Mrs. Marcel: I'm interested in Psychology. My brother is a ... well he's a doctor... was I should say, is a doctor. He was wondering... you know... when he was beginning to study. "Why," he said, "Do I have to take that Psychology for?" I said, "That's going to be one of the most important subjects you've taken."

Linda: So you have two doctors in the family? You have an uncle and a son?

Jesse: Her brother is a doctor. Our son is a doctor. And my nephew is... he's not a doctor, he's a dentist.

THE APPENDECTOMY

Jesse: Oh, I've got something else to tell you.

Linda: I knew if I'd stick around long enough you'd tell me something that's not in the book.

Jesse: No, this is not in the book. You won't want to make notes on that either.

Linda: Oh, yes I will.

For The Sake of My Country

Jesse: When I was in combat, we were stationed on the island of Owe out in the West Indies.

[I am not sure of the spelling of this island. I have spelled it the way it sounded on the tape. Jesse had mentioned that he had been in New Guinea in the Pacific, so one might assume that he meant the Pacific Islands and not the West Indies. There is an island located north of New Guinea called Iwo, however, I am not sure if this is the location he spoke of. If it is not, then possibly he meant one of the Hawaiian Islands.]

Our flight surgeon who was a Dr. Nathan Goustack. He's from...

Mrs. Marcel: Oh, oh. Here it comes.

Linda: What? What?

Mrs. Marcel: The operation.

Jesse: I had to do an appendectomy. Linda, you can do anything you have to do. It's simple. It's a mechanical thing.

HYPNOTIC REGRESSION

Linda: Tell me how you feel about things like psychology, hypnosis, and ESP and all of that?

Jesse: Oh, I believe in it. I believe in it.

Linda: Have you ever been hypnotized?

Jesse: No.

Linda: Would you consider it?

Jesse: If I could do somebody some good, yes I'd consider it.

Mrs. Marcel: Ha! You'd better not. You'd probably tell them the truth.

[I intentionally did not address the statements made concerning "lies" or "the truth" even though it appeared that the Marcels wanted me to.]

Jesse: You know a person that can be hypnotized has to have a flexible mind.

Linda: The word hypnosis has a stigma attached to it. A lot of people are afraid of it. It's nothing to be afraid of. You're in control. You think the therapist is, but you are. But it still has a stigma attached to it. Anyway, I was going to ask you how you felt about it.

Jesse: Oh, I believe in it.

Linda: But you know, through hypnosis... while you're... after several sessions when you get used to the therapist, he can make you go back and remember things that are kind of fuzzy. And maybe under hypnosis you could remember exactly what the Hieroglyphs were and you can write them down and we could have definite proof. (Laughter)

Mrs. Marcel: Oh, well, you remember something that you didn't even pay too much attention to at the time.

Linda: I'm saying that you would have a pencil in your hand and a paper in your hand. This would be after several sessions when you get comfortable. So he could bring you back to that exact moment.

Mrs. Marcel: That's what I'm interested in... is taking you back [in time]. I just wonder... you know... I was just one of those passers by.

Linda: And when you make your autobiography that would go... it would be something not in here [*The Roswell Incident* book]. You'd have something extra.

Jesse: You mean I could be on the Today program and advertise a book. (Laughter)

Linda: Sure you could. And let me tell you the money would come in so fast...

Jesse: The money is something I don't want.

Mrs. Marcel: Oh well.

Linda: What do you want, then?

Jesse: Peace in life.

[I think Jesse wanted peace from his past. Peace from the secrets that he held for so long. Some secrets that he had just begun to share with others and some that he most likely took to his grave.]

Figure 6

Linda Corley, Ph.D.

Linda: You've got peace. It's so peaceful here. You don't feel like that?

Jesse: Well, I've got what I want right here.

Mrs. Marcel: My brother says we have a paradise on earth right here.

Jesse: We've got everything.

Linda: It's very peaceful here. So you already have what you want.

Jesse: I already have what I want. Why should I want more?

[It sounded like he was asking himself that question and I'm not sure he knew the answer.]

Linda: Then why are you thinking about writing a book?

Jesse: Not for my own good. For the good of other people who might… who know what somebody else had to do with their life.

[Was he looking for someone else who had kept hidden secret burdens? Through the catharsis of writing a book, maybe he could have found peace.]

Linda: You would be helping. You would be contributing of yourself.

Jesse: I'd be helping them.

Linda: Right. That's right.

Jesse: Now that's what I've got in mind.

[Jesse never seemed to want anything for himself. He put his concern for others ahead of his own. He never did write that book. And I believe that he never did divulge all of his secrets.]

Linda: Don't you think that through... maybe this one link... that you have with the Hieroglyphs... I feel like that is so important. I know I'm harping on it but I feel like that is a clue to what we've lost. Only the USAF has, and we may never know. Only through what you saw written on that piece of wood could maybe be deciphered now 30 years later. We have physicists who might know now.

Jesse: Linda, they have all that stuff. It's in laboratories. They've analyzed those things to the Nth degree. Can I help them?

Linda: They have the stuff. That's considering they still have it.

Jesse: They have studied it.

Linda: So, I guess it is true that they still have it then. We have to assume they still have it.

Jesse: I think they still have it. Cause nothing has ever been let out by the Air Force of any materials that I ever picked up. They had materials there that I had never seen before.

Linda: OK, then, you're the link. You're the link to that. You have seen them. And under hypnosis you could write down what you saw, exactly the way you saw it.

Jesse: She [wife] could write down what she saw, too. Our son could do the same thing.

[Twelve years later, in 1993, under hypnosis, their son Jesse Jr. would draw his version of what he remembered of the Hieroglyphic writing. This version is much different than what his father drew for me during this interview. You can draw your own conclusions about this. Of course there is the possibility that the different beams had different writings on each of them. Or, the fact that an event can be viewed by many people who remember, report, and interpret it in many different ways.]

Linda: That's right. All three of ya'll could, through hypnosis.

Mrs. Marcel: Well Jesse, little Jesse tried to draw...

Linda: Yeah, but through hypnosis, he could. He could draw exactly what he saw through hypnosis.

[In my own, quite obvious way, I was trying to set up the scenario for the Marcels to agree to be hypnotized by a friend of mine from the local university.]

Mrs. Marcel: Well that was an odd thing. I was just one of those people... I'd just pass by now and then... you know... wishing they'd hurry up and get out.

Linda: Get out your kitchen?

Mrs. Marcel: Get out of my kitchen. I looked at that stuff and, "Jimminie Christmas, that looks like some kind of Hieroglyphics." And then they started looking.

Linda: God, I wish I could've seen it.

Jesse: I wish you would have been there.

[Jesse's tone in that statement was forlorn. It was uttered in a whisper as he reflected back to that time and the events that have since transpired. It was almost like he would have wanted a witness, other than his family, to validate what happened to him.]

DREAMS

Jesse: I want to tell you one dream I had. It was a repetitious dream. I dreamed of my own mother. And she lived in a three room house along a stream, right by the main highway. I can even remember the paved road to her house. I dreamed that. Not one time but several times. The same dream. The stream was very deep. There were some big fish in that stream and she lived there. This is a three room house. And every time I would dream of her... she's living there... I could visit her.

For The Sake of My Country

Linda: You visited your mother in your dreams? That's fantastic.

Jesse: Yeah. She died at the age of 102 years of age. She died when our son finished medical school. In 1961, I think. She was born in 1859. My daddy died when he was 69 years old. Younger than I am now. I was in St. Louis when he died. He was sick when I left here.

Mrs. Marcel: He had a stroke.

Jesse: Well anyway, he died and I was in St. Louis. I was staying... I was going to school in St. Louis. And that evening on a Friday, I took off and went to Chicago. And while I was in Chicago, he died. And when I came back there was a telegram saying my daddy had died.

Linda: So you came back here?

Jesse: No. It was no use. By the time I'd get back here, he would've already been buried. So my mother was there and she moved to my sister's house.

Linda: How many brothers and sisters do you have?

Jesse: In my family there were 9. I'm the last one. My younger sister is 81. I have another sister 91. They live right here on Bayou Blue.

Mrs. Marcel: I took the 81 year old out today.

Jesse: She went to the beauty shop.

Linda: What about your grandparents?

Jesse: The grandparents on my father's side... I never kept up with them. My grandparents on my mother's side, I did. They were pretty old when they died. I was just a kid.

Mrs. Marcel: If Jesse took care of himself, he could live to be 150.

81

Linda Corley, Ph.D.

Linda: Gotta stop that smoking. But you only smoke because you don't have anything to do.

Jesse: It's my only out.

Mrs. Marcel: He's got to do something with his hands.

HAM RADIO HOBBY

Jesse: Let me tell you something else. I'm an amateur radio... I'm a licensed amateur radio operator.

Linda: You need to get a HAM set.

Mrs.. Marcel: He has one.

Linda: He does?

Jesse: A HAM set! I've got one. I've got a first rate operation there. You know the reason I don't get on the air? Every time I talk to somebody, they want to talk about this [*The Roswell Incident* book].

Linda: Well, don't tell them who you are.

Jesse: They know who I am. I give my call sign.

Linda: What's your call sign?

Jesse: W5CYI. I've had that call letter since 1930. I'll tell you what I did. You remember when we had guys walking on the moon? One of them, I talked to, directly. I've got cards to verify that. And you know when they retrieved the...[space capsule] I talked to the ship. They were just recovering the bodies coming back from outer space. And I took a message from him for somebody in New Orleans. And I got on the telephone and I called somebody in New Orleans. So you see, I've been active.

Linda: You still talk on your radio?

Jesse: Oh, yes. I can talk all over the world.

Linda: That's a great hobby.

Jesse: You met somebody more than you thought you'd meet.

Linda: No. You're really living up to my expectations. You really are. That's a great hobby. It just doesn't keep you busy enough though, huh?

Jesse: I lost interest in HAM radio operator cause I'll tell you what. Every time I talk to somebody, they want to discuss this. And I don't want to discuss that on the air with anybody. But that's all they want to talk about.

Linda: Well, just tell them you can't and then talk to somebody else.

Jesse: I just don't know. I listen to it.

Linda: I enjoyed you telling me about the book but I enjoy listening to you talk about yourself more than the book. Do you understand that?

Jesse: Maybe so. I'm not that interesting.

Linda: I find you are.

Jesse: I want to take you back there. I'll show you my whole HAM station. I can put 2,000 watts on the air and talk to anybody I want to throughout the world.

Linda: I never saw one.

Jesse: You never?

Linda: No. So, we're gonna go?

Linda Corley, Ph.D.

[Recorder off for tour of radio room in back room of his house. When we returned to the kitchen, Mrs. Marcel turned the television on to watch the six o'clock news.]

Jesse: Channel 4 News is coming on at six.

Mrs. Marcel: I could offer you a beer.

Linda: Oh, thank you, no. I've had enough just sitting here drinking that wine.

CHAPTER FOUR
A HOME REMEMBERED

> When we were in Roswell, we were busy people. Listen, I barely remembered where I lived, I was so busy there.
>
> ~~ JESSE MARCEL, SR.

ROSWELL REVISITED

Linda: So you went last month, which was April, to film with…

Jesse: Yes, with Johnny Mann and his Eye Witness News.

Linda: OK, before that, when was the last time you went to Roswell?

Jesse: The year before with Landsberg Productions to go and make a movie for them. Now, that movie was supposed to be out across country. They showed it on about 50 TV stations.

Mrs. Marcel: You know, like the show "That's Incredible?"

Jesse: Well, I hadn't been back over there. They came over here and filmed me here. That was International Group One that came over here.

Linda: When was the time before that… you went to Roswell?

Linda Corley, Ph.D.

Jesse: Well, I went year before last and last year.

Linda: And that's it?

Jesse: That's it.

Linda: Besides the 30 years ago?

Jesse: Yeah. But Roswell has changed so much. Good God. It's a clean town.

Mrs. Marcel: When we lived there...

Jesse: Linda, you can go there... you can park your car at a grocery store... you can leave the keys on the ignition switch. You don't have to worry about it.

Mrs. Marcel: Don't have to worry about anybody stealing it.

Linda: Do you have any pictures of when you all were in Roswell? In the family photo album... something I can look at?

Jesse: I don't think we have.

Linda: You all didn't take any pictures?

Mrs. Marcel: We didn't have time.

Jesse: No. When we were in Roswell we were busy people. Listen, I barely remembered where I lived when I... I was so busy there.

Mrs. Marcel: I had a Bridge Club and the Cub Scouts and that was it. Every now and then a party.

Jesse: You know what... this Johnny Mann, Channel 4? We went to this house that she and I lived in. It's been changed over. But he had to take me to the kitchen where I had brought the stuff in. Of course, the kitchen is no longer where it used to be. But they took pictures of my feet on the kitchen floor.

DR. JESSE MARCEL JR.

Mrs. Marcel: Linda, the cutest thing, though, is when they were interviewing little Jesse. He was sitting in that chair over there and it's a rocking chair. Of course he was rocking and rocking. The photographer says, "There's just one thing I want to ask you. Please don't rock." He said, "When you do your head goes up and down and you look funny."

Linda: How old is little Jesse now?

Mrs. Marcel: Oh Lord, he's 40 what?

Jesse: Forty five.

Mrs. Marcel: No he's not 45.

Jesse: He's 44.

Mrs. Marcel: You see, he was 11 when all this happened.

Linda: Why did he choose Montana?

Jesse: He loves to ski.

Mrs. Marcel: He's got some Indian blood.

Jesse: He's got a beautiful home out there. He's got two children.

Linda: You all must miss him.

Mrs. Marcel: You know, he lost his wife the other day. She was killed in an automobile accident.

Jesse: On the 12th of November.

Mrs. Marcel: They had only been married 17 years.

Jesse: Big 18 wheeler just smashed her.

Mrs. Marcel: When I went over there, they had a bunch of these cards [referring to the funeral]. There was one that was written on this yellow paper you know what... lined paper. I read the whole thing and I said, "That's had to be written by an Indian." And he looked at the name and he said, "Momma, it was."

Jesse: Our son is an Ear, Nose, and Throat Specialist. An E.N.T. Incidentally, he went to Nicholls [local university].

Linda: Has he thought of coming back here, since she's gone?

Mrs. Marcel: He thought of it, but he says there's just too much traffic and he doesn't want to move the kids. He's got two kids. It's been hard.

Linda: When is he coming back to visit?

Jesse: He'll be here in September.

Linda: That's not too far. Can I meet him?

Jesse: Yeah, you certainly can.

Linda: OK, I'm gonna call you all. Or maybe you all could call me. Let me leave you my number.

[I gave the Marcels my phone number.]

Mrs. Marcel: He's supposed to come back in September.

Jesse: He's going to Fort Rucker Alabama for Helicopter Pilot training. He's a Lt. Col. in the Air Force himself.

Mrs. Marcel: Why would he want to do that? I mean, that's dangerous.

Linda: It must be the closest feeling to flying in a UFO cause it goes straight up into the air.

For The Sake of My Country

Mrs. Marcel: Well, you know that little Jesse... he and his two sons were going to town. And all of a sudden, one of them says, "Daddy look." There was something. He actually did see one [UFO], up in Montana.

Linda: Well, do you... things that happened in your life... all these years... have you kept up on readings?

Jesse: Not too much.

Mrs. Marcel: He hasn't done anything like that. I do all the reading in this family.

[Here again, a mention of Jesse not reading. It is possible that Mrs. Marcel related what she read to Jesse because of his poor eyesight.]

Linda: So you're not even interested that much?

Jesse: I became disinterested.

Linda: You became disinterested... because they abused it so much?

Jesse: There's something wrong within me, you see. And I know that.

[I now feel that he literally meant that there was something within himself that he was struggling with.]

Linda: You feel there's something wrong with you cause of that [Roswell incident]?

Jesse: No. I'm still... I'm still curious.

Linda: But you're not reading.

Jesse: I'm not reading. You know the reason why I'm not reading? The reason I'm not reading... I've had enough to do with the news media in my life. Cause if you give the news media one paragraph, the next day you're gonna read two columns written on the very

Linda Corley, Ph.D.

subject, the next day. So when you read the newspaper, you read about 3% facts. All the rest is malarkey.

[I wish I would have asked what exactly happened between him and the news media during his lifetime.]

Linda: Well, that's why... in the book... you said a lot of the stuff is right but then a lot of it's not. Cause they stretch it?

Jesse: Right. A lot of the stuff is authentic... something that I know. I have something I want to tell you. See, when I was an officer my office was in the Selective Service building. I had a big office there. I had an officer working for me. She was in charge of picking up the briefing room cause I had to brief people... including the President of Brazil and President Truman. I mingled with big people. And my immediate Commanding Officer was a two star General, General Nelson.

SPECIAL WEAPONS DEVELOPMENT

Jesse: I was assigned to an organization called the Special Weapons Development Program.

Linda: And what were the special weapons?

Jesse: I'm not going to tell you. (Laughter) My job was to monitor. We had to be sent all around the world collecting air samples. To collect any form of radio activity in the air.

Linda: Cause of the bomb?

Jesse: Yeah. That came through my office. And I had to be the director of the naval research laboratory. It was my job to collect all the air samples they got and take them to the Naval Research Laboratory and have them analyzed.

Linda: And were they radioactive?

Jesse: Well, one was.

Linda: Where was it at?

Jesse: It was picked up on the _____Island, out of Alaska. And we know exactly where that Atomic device was exploded. It was exploded by Russia [in 1949]. It was picked up on the base. I got the samples and brought them to NRL and had them analyzed. That night my telephone rang. The guy at NRL told me, "Get yourself out here." And I went out there. They had Shore Patrol... in the Navy you use Shore Patrol instead of MPs. He was guarding. I told him who I was. I got in. He said, "Now I'll show you a report." He says, "You look at it. Go back to your office and you can write me a report, cause you have information I don't have." They had definite indications that the Russians had exploded an Atomic device, because of the particles in the air. I came back from the office. I didn't even give it to my secretary. I typed a message myself to the Military General and I showed it to him. I'm telling you something that was never published. Even the Washington Post never got it. (Laughter)

[It appears that he meant that he had not stated this information in any previous interview.]

Mrs. Marcel: If the Washington Post didn't get it...

Jesse: All right. Well, this is what happened. That was at 4 o'clock in the morning. I turned the report over to the General. He says, "Fine." I says, "I'm leaving this with you." He says, "You have to leave it with me." So he called superiors. And you know that pouch? Well, he sent it... I know it was sent to CIA, that evening... that very evening. President Truman came on the air that they had definite proof that the Russians had exploded an Atomic device.

Linda: And that was through your work and your efforts?

Jesse: Word for word, the way I wrote it. President Truman announced that on the air... radio and television. See, that was my job. That's why they called it Special Weapons Development.

Linda Corley, Ph.D.

Linda: But at the time that you were doing all of this… they kept you busy in Washington. And after they got you and pulled you from Roswell, you didn't think that they were trying to keep your mind occupied so you wouldn't continue thinking about it [Roswell incident]?

Jesse: Yeah. I always felt that way. That's right.

Linda: Couldn't you kick yourself now for not going to try to find out more stuff?

Jesse: No.

Linda: No? But you had a foot in the door already.

Jesse: I performed my duty.

Linda: They say that you helped cover up? You wouldn't talk. But that's not covering up. That's just not saying nothing. Well, I guess in a way you did [cover up].

Jesse: I just didn't talk about something I wasn't supposed to talk about.

Mrs. Marcel: When you're told not to talk about it… and you are working for the government…

Linda: Oh yeah, but you see the way they make it sound? I'm just a lay person but I feel they're making you sound like one of the enemy.

Jesse: That's because I was part of the Air Force.

Mrs. Marcel: He couldn't talk.

Jesse: I did exactly what I had to do.

[The conversation was interrupted when our attention went to the television set. Channel 4 News was presenting "Contact UFO," a week

long series by New Orleans reporter Johnny Mann. It reported that Jesse Marcel would be on "tomorrow night's segment."]

Linda: All right, tomorrow night is going to be the good one. (Laughter)

Mrs. Marcel: I hope so. I hope we get it.

[The news report went on to say that reporter Johnny Mann interviewed Calvin Parker in Golden Meadow, Louisiana where he had been living for the last few years. Parker had admitted that he had been abducted aboard a UFO. On October 11, 1973, at 9 p.m., Charles Hickson, 42, and Calvin Parker, 19, were fishing on a pier in Pascagoula, Mississippi near the Shaupeter Shipyard. They heard a buzzing behind them, turned around and were terrified to see an approximately 10-foot-wide, 8-foot-high, glowing egg-shaped object with blue lights hovering above the ground about 40 feet away. As they watched, a door appeared at the bottom of the object and three gray-skinned creatures floated out. The aliens were about five feet tall, had bullet-shaped heads without necks, slits for mouths and conical structures sticking out where their noses and ears would be. They also had rounded feet, clawed hands and no eyes. Two of the beings grabbed Hickson, while the third grabbed Parker. The 19 year old immediately fainted from fright. Hickson, who remained conscious, claimed that the creatures floated them into a brightly lit room aboard the UFO. The two men were examined with some sort of electronic eye that Hickson reported hung in mid-air with no visible connection to any other part of the compartment. Twenty minutes after the incredible events began, Hickson and Parker were returned to the riverside. The UFO rose straight into the air and shot out of sight. They said that none of the creatures communicated with them; the only sound coming from the aliens was buzzing. To this day, Hickson believes that the mechanical-like movements and buzzing indicates the abductors were robots. Parker, now 47, lives in Texas. Hickson is 70 and currently resides in Gautier, Mississippi.]

CHAPTER FIVE
A SANCTUARY FOR ALL

> What is national security today? Now security means that every politician in Washington has to know all of it. And they shouldn't!
> ~ JESSE MARCEL, SR.

CALVIN PARKER

Linda: Can you imagine Calvin Parker living in Golden Meadow, Louisiana?

Jesse: I'd like to meet him.

Linda: Can I bring him here?

Jesse: Why sure.

Mrs. Marcel: That would be fun.

[I did find Calvin Parker and I did speak with him concerning the experience he had in Pascagoula, Mississippi. He and I met many times and he was willing to meet with the Marcels, however I did not bring them together due to the phone call I received from Jesse. Calvin introduced me to Betty Hill, via the telephone. She was also interested in speaking to Jesse, especially about the writing on the craft beams.]

Jesse: I'd like to talk to him.

For The Sake of My Country

Linda: I have a feeling if you got together... if he could get with some people who believe in...

Mrs. Marcel: That old man Hickson... I don't know...

Linda: I know. But... you saw... they took the polygraph test?

Jesse: Yeah.

Linda: And they passed it.

Jesse: Yeah.

Linda: I guess you gotta be kind of... detach yourself from it. I can't do that.

Mrs. Marcel: That's the way Jesse was. When he went to Roswell and went into this house... and this one couple was so glad...

Jesse: Oh Lord. Those people....

Mrs. Marcel: That was our home. We had bought and paid for it.

Jesse: They invited me into that house with open arms. I could see every change that was made in the kitchen. They added two rooms behind that. How they widened the back door.

Linda: Was the cement slab still out there?

Jesse: It was still there.

Linda: Do you feel there's something under that slab?

Jesse: I don't think so. I'll tell you the reason why. Cause when I brought the stuff... it was after 1946... 1946 when I laid the slab. You know the reason why we laid the slab out there? I bought a Bendix washing machine. We didn't have room in the kitchen to put it. I put a cement slab out there. We put it there and whenever it would get down to 30 degrees above zero the water would freeze and she couldn't wash. But that was 1946 when I came back from the Pacific.

Linda: Boy, I wish it wouldn't have been. I wish you all would have...

Jesse: Oh, they were ready to get somebody to get a contractor to tear up the whole house and take the concrete out.

Linda: And you told them different?

Jesse: Yeah, cause I remember I laid the slab before I brought the UFO stuff. I say UFO stuff, whatever it was.

[Jesse was the first to admit that his memory of those past events was not as sharp as he would like them to be. However, he was adamant about this concrete slab. Why not let them dig up the slab? If somebody is willing to foot the bill, what would it hurt? It would surely put that one question to rest, one way or the other.]

MEETING WITH PAUL WILMOT

Linda: Surely you have a feeling about it. That's your feeling. You feel it is a UFO. I feel it's a UFO and I didn't even see the stuff.

Jesse: Well, the thing is... I talked to the son of a man who actually saw it explode.

Mrs. Marcel: Oh yeah, that's Wilmot.

Jesse: He runs the TV station in Roswell.

Mrs. Marcel: This man actually saw the thing explode in the air. And his son works for a TV station in Roswell.

Jesse: See, the son, he made a complete recording of what he [the father] saw... what he and his wife saw that evening.

For The Sake of My Country

Linda: Whose got that recording?

Jesse: The man I know in Roswell has that.

Linda: Did you tell Berlitz and Moore?

Jesse: No. There's a hell of a lot that I haven't said.

[I wish I had asked him to elaborate on this statement. But, somehow, I feel that there is indeed a whole lot more that Jesse kept to himself about the incident and was never going to tell.]

Jesse: Now Mr. Paul Wilmot, I met him... He's the advertising agent for KBI TV Roswell. A mighty important television station. I met the gentleman. The first time I met him is when I went over there. When I was with... that was Landsberg Productions... that I was with in Roswell. We went to his house. We met the man. I talked to this gentleman and he told that to Landsberg Productions. That his daddy had related the whole thing to him... what he saw that very night that it happened... that object. He said it was due southwest of Roswell. He said it waited... it... took off fast and exploded. Now he and his wife were on the front porch at night. He [Paul Wilmot] has the whole works. They interviewed Paul Wilmot and they even took a picture... a close up picture... a beautiful picture of Mr. Dan Wilmot and they put it on the land and photographed it. And they carried it in that film that they made. They filmed Mr. Paul Wilmot, too. And that's when I met Paul Wilmot. He was about as nice a gentleman as you'll want to meet. The son is the one I talked to. That's twice I've met him already. And he's still living there. He told me the whole works. He told me everything. Now I've spent a lot of time with the man. I like him. For one thing, he's one of the most likable gentlemen you've ever met in your life. He's a salesman, actually. He sells commercials for the station. But he also runs the station. And so that's how I got to know the Wilmots. Not Dan, the one who saw it, cause he's dead now... been dead. But his daddy told him... his dad and mother told him everything that they watched. And they saw it explode and about two or three days later some rancher came

Linda Corley, Ph.D.

into Roswell and told the Sheriff about it. That's when I got called out there [Roswell in 1947].

Linda: Do you feel like there was... something about a lightning storm... that it could have been a lightning storm?

Jesse: There was lightning. There was bad weather that night. But the man who originally called in said he heard a big boom. He didn't know if it was thunder or what it was. The next day is when he wandered around and found all the debris.

Linda: They just speculated that it exploded right there and then it kept going over the mountains and then it crashed and that's the stuff you found?

Jesse: Right. Where it exploded in Roswell, some of the stuff fell. That's where I went to.

Linda: Well, I sure wish you'd have been the one on the other side of that mountain. Good grief. The whole craft. You would probably, right now, know exactly where the craft was.

Mrs. Marcel: That's where they were supposed to have found the beings or whatever they were.

Linda: Well, you know they're going to have to have beings if the craft was operating. Somebody's got to drive it.

Mrs. Marcel: It could've been operated mechanically.

Linda: That's true.

Jesse: Well, it's hard to know this whole thing. In other words... I'll tell you... I was so busy... the business that I was doing. I had a lot of responsibility. After all, I had 5 officers. I had a Major, a Captain, and 3 Lieutenants working for me. And 3 counter-intelligence agents working for me. I was running a big investigating...

Linda: And they make you a Lt. Col. and you don't even want to stay in the Army [Air Force]. And you leave the Army and you don't even know you're a Lt. Col. (Laughter)

Jesse: I had 20 typewriters working for me all the time. Electric typewriters...

Mrs. Marcel: No you didn't have 20 typewriters working. Somebody was working them.

[Mrs. Marcel operated somewhat as Jesse's conscience.]

Jesse: I had 10 typewriters in operation but 20 typists. They would alternate. That was my job. I had to sign so many papers that I'd get writer's cramp just to sign my signature. I even had a stamp. I'd just stamp those things.

Linda: All the wood and tin and aluminum foil and Hieroglyphs was really interfering with your business.

Jesse: It was interfering with my job. So I didn't pay that much attention to it.

Linda: Do you think now that you wish you would've paid more attention to it.

Jesse: Yeah. I wish I would have.

Mrs. Marcel: I wish I would have grabbed a little piece of it.

DESCRIPTION OF DEBRIS

Jesse: But the material was unusual. Of course the Air Force called it a balloon. It couldn't have been. It was porous. It couldn't hold any air.

Linda: Was there anything that looked like a balloon? I mean, anybody can tell a balloon from a....

Jesse: The material was fabric... the material. I tried to blow through it. It would go right through it. And you see, a balloon has to have... has to be...

Linda: What did you try to blow through?

[At this point, I did not recall any fabric and was curious about his description.]

Jesse: I tried to blow it with my mouth.

Linda: What piece? That foil looking stuff?

Jesse: No, no. The actual... what looked like balloon material. A cloth.

Linda: OK, cloth. You tried to blow through the cloth and you could blow right through it.

Jesse: Oh, Lord. It wouldn't hold any air.

Linda: It had cloth, too. Now you see, you didn't tell me anything about cloth.

Jesse: Well, it's a cloth like material, but it was also metallic.

[Now I was really confused. This statement had me baffled then and now. I thought that the metal was the stuff that could not be folded, wrinkled, or bent with a sledge hammer.]

Linda: Oh, it was a metallic cloth?

Jesse: It was a metallic cloth. It would go right through it. I even tried to burn it. It wouldn't burn.

[This was the description initially given for the foil-like material.]

Linda: Wouldn't burn? Can you burn a balloon?

Jesse: You bet you can. See, a balloon has to have... halogen [sic] or other gas to go up in the air... even hot air. This could not hold anything like that. It was porous.

Linda: Was most of the material... the wood, the tin, or the material... that you picked up... What was the most?

Jesse: I guess there was most of... the material. As much as I can remember it. I couldn't spend enough time with it to really analyze anything.

Linda: And all the balloons... other balloons you've seen... they didn't have stuff like that wood and the Hieroglyphic stuff?

Jesse: Hell no!

Linda: I still want to find out more about them Hieroglyphs. And you got it in your head. You've [Mrs. Marcel] got it in your head, too.

Mrs. Marcel: I don't really think so. I didn't pay that too much attention.

Jesse: And so has my son.

Linda: He [Jesse, Sr.] probably saw a little bit more... and your son [Jesse, Jr..] saw a bit more than you [Mrs. Marcel] did.

Jesse: Well, it's a strange thing.

Linda: I just feel that's [writing on beam] holding a lot of information. And I know that you say there are physicists and scientists are all studying that stuff right now undercover with the US Air Force... but...

Jesse: Incidentally, there's something else I can tell you. We... here's something...

Linda Corley, Ph.D.

Linda: Feel free to tell me anything.

Jesse: They tried their best... you know Barry Goldwater? He's a 4 Star General in the Air Force. He tried to get permission to go look at this stuff. And he was refused permission to look at it. If it wasn't a cover up, what was it?

Mrs. Marcel: That's the only thing that makes me believe it might have been something, was because of the cover up.

OTHER UFOs SIGHTED BY MARCEL

Jesse: There's something else I didn't tell you, cause it doesn't amount to anything. One night, at 11:30 at night, I was living in town. The Provost Marshal called me. And the Provost Marshal was under me for security. Now he had his own job as a Military Policeman. He had his own MP uniform. He called me at 11:30 at night. Said, "You'd better get your so-and-so out here."

[Jesse never makes it clear why he was called out with such urgency. It appears that it was because of UFO activity in the area.]

Jesse: I got in the Buck and I floor-boarded it. Four miles through town to the Air Base. And while I was driving as fast as I can drive, the Buick can go 85 miles per hour wide open, I saw 6 objects right over my head, in formation but much faster than any aircraft that we had could fly.

Mrs. Marcel: I wish I could have seen that.

[This was said in a most sincere tone of voice. It made me feel that she was almost envious of Jesse's sighting.]

Jesse: In about two seconds it had gone beyond the horizon and I didn't think nothing about it. When I got to the base, I'll never forget this Major Edwin Easley, he's the Provost Marshal. He's the one who called me, said, "Did you see that?" I said, "See what?" "Did you see those things go through?" I said, "Yeah."

Linda: He had seen them, too?

Jesse: Yeah. He'd seen them. They went right over my head. And before I could blink my eyes, they were out of sight.

Linda: And they didn't know what it was?

[I assumed that radar would have identified whatever it was.]

Jesse: No.

Linda: Did you all hear anything more...

Jesse: We didn't discuss that anymore.

Linda: You didn't discuss it anymore?

[This surprised me. No mention was made as to whether or not this was reported. Wouldn't it be protocol for an Intelligence Officer on an Air Force base to report UFO activity in his area? Or is this some of the information that Jesse was still keeping to himself?]

Jesse: No.

Mrs. Marcel: Well, you see Linda. If we'd ever see it [UFO], we would know [to report it].

Linda: If you or I would see something we would discuss it till you could not discuss it anymore. And these people see it and don't say nothing!

Mrs. Marcel: We wouldn't give up would we?

Linda: I would badger them [military] to death. (Laughter)

Jesse: We're a different breed, that's why.

Linda Corley, Ph.D.

Linda: You all are so brainwashed into not believing this because it's not logical.

Jesse: It's not not believing. We were brainwashed into keeping what you see and what you hear, in your head.

[I was surprised he admitted to the brainwashing aspect, however, this statement is in keeping with his remarks about keeping things like this to yourself.]

Mrs. Marcel: Well, if I ever see it [UFO] I'll let you know. (Laughter)

NATIONAL SECURITY

Linda: What does the statement 'In the interest of National Security' mean to you? That's what they keep saying. Don't say anything. Keep quiet because it's in the interest of national security. What does that mean?

Jesse: Well, it used to mean something. Today, it don't. What is national security today? Now security means that every politician in Washington has to know all of it. And they shouldn't!

Linda: You feel they shouldn't?

Jesse: I feel they shouldn't.

Linda: You feel the Air Force really should have a top... a lid on all this and control it.

Jesse: That's right. I feel that way, yeah. Cause I was trained by the Air Force. Incidentally, I was in Intelligence School. There's something else I want to tell you. My commanding officer was a German Intelligence Officer. And my instructors were British Intelligence Officers. We had no "Intelligence" in this country, when I went to Intelligence School.

Linda: You were taught by the best.

Jesse: Right. I feel that way.

Linda: But you honestly feel that National Security would have been endangered by you telling the news media that you really saw this [UFO]?

Jesse: Yeah. I believe this.

Linda: How?

Jesse: The thing is that they thought that it was necessary that nothing be said about it and I aligned with them.

Mrs. Marcel: Now you see, I would have done the same thing, if they would have told me to.

[This is probably a typical cross-sectional response of people in this country when it comes to following orders of their leaders. I, as a child of the 1960s, had a lot of trouble with the concept of blindly following the wishes of government officials.]

Jesse: My own wife didn't know half the things I did.

Mrs. Marcel: And I'm sure glad I didn't.

Jesse: Sometimes I'd leave... I didn't tell her anything about it. Like the day I went on that mission to pick up all that stuff. She didn't know where I was. And I was gone overnight.

[Indicating that he did not spend that night at home.]

Linda: Were you upset by it [UFO crash site] personally?

Jesse: No.

Linda: You didn't feel...

Jesse: I was very calm.

Linda: 'This is something from another world and I'm scared.' You didn't feel that way?

Jesse: You go through that... you don't think. You don't have a thought in your mind.

[More results of brainwashing?]

Mrs. Marcel: You're just there... when it happened.

Linda: Well, if you just picked up remains of a craft... you didn't feel somebody was outside of there... right there... you know... none of that?

Mrs. Marcel: No dead bodies.

Linda: I wonder how you would have felt if you would have seen dead bodies?

Jesse: I would have picked them up and brought them in.

Linda: But that would have changed your life. Surely, that would have to change the rest of your life?

Jesse: Well, I think many things have changed my life. To give you an idea... very quick. When I first reported for duty overseas, my main job there was photographic interpretation, not combat intelligence officer. I went and opened the Bombay's of a B-25 when it had just come in and a dead body full of blood fell all over me.

Linda: Must have been tough for you, huh?

Jesse: I picked up... it really didn't... I just picked him up and we put him in the ambulance. You are devoted to your work. And when you are devoted to your work, whatever your work is, you do it. Without question.

Linda: I don't know. I think if somebody told me, "Linda you can't tell nobody that you just took a ride on that UFO." I mean, I think I'd have to tell somebody. If they said it would endanger my country, I'd still have to say it. "Look, I did it. I saw it." (Laughter)

Jesse: I don't think you would.

Mrs. Marcel: Well, I think that it more or less depends on... not... I wouldn't say brainwash...

Linda: It would scare me to think that you wouldn't believe me. Like these men from Pascagoula, they're going through a lot of problems right now.

Jesse: I know they are.

Linda: And he [Calvin Parker] feels he's still communicating...

Jesse: Well, that's what he said.

[This was said in a somewhat skeptical tone of voice.]

Mrs. Marcel: Yeah, but what if somebody decided they wanted to communicate with you just because you're talking about it?

[Referring to the Men In Black who some believe could be alien themselves or government agents.]

Linda: You may be contacted. You will let me know, won't you? You've got my phone number.

[I felt that since Jesse had decided to come out and tell his story, there may be a possibility that he would receive a visit from the MIBs.]

Mrs. Marcel: You know, I thought of that.

[She seemed to have given some thought to the possibility of MIBs contacting Jesse.]

Linda Corley, Ph.D.

PHOTOS OF MARCELS TAKEN

Linda: Hey, yeah, I know… one more request. Can I have a picture?

Jesse: You're gonna break the camera. (Laughter) I don't mind. I've been photographed more in the past two years…

Mrs.. Marcel: Do you want us together?

Linda: Yes.

Jesse: Move over on this side.

Linda: Come on Mom. Go sit with Dad. (Laughter)

Mrs. Marcel: OK, daughter. (Laughter)

[In a short period of time, we had become comfortable enough to jokingly refer to one another as "Mom" and "daughter."]

(Three photos were taken.)

For The Sake of My Country

Figure 7

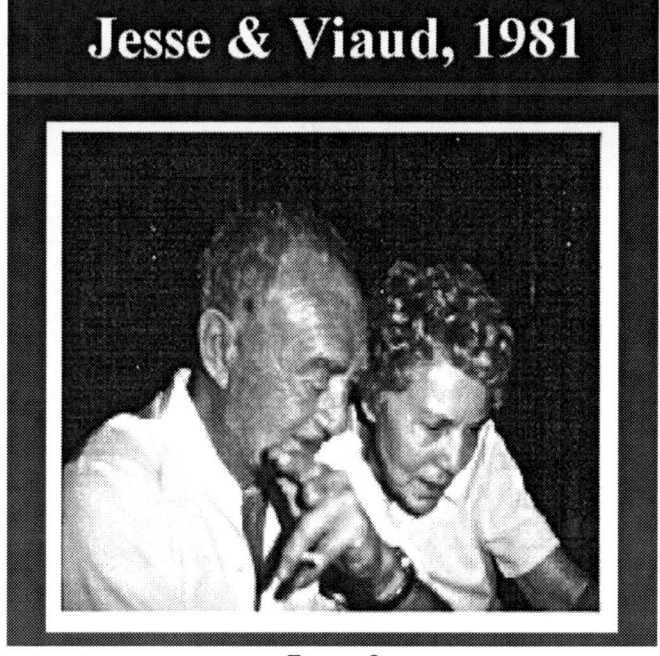

Figure 8

Linda Corley, Ph.D.

Me and Jesse, 1981

Figure 9

CHAPTER SIX
A NEED FOR SOLITUDE

You get to an age where you have to settle down.
~ JESSE MARCEL, SR.

HOLLYWOOD LIFE

Jesse: I'll tell you one thing. I will tell you this now. I'd like to go to California and work with Carroll O'Connor. He's not all what you see on TV.

Linda: What's stopping you?

Jesse: We have a lot of property here. We have pets. There's a lot of work to do. It would be hard to just take off. We've done that before in our lives. You get to an age where you have to settle down.

Mrs. Marcel: I told him to go and I'd stay here and take care of the pets and he can send me the $10,000 a week.

Jesse: You have to be on a movie set for 10 - 15 hours a day working and taking direction. I've worked under a director already. And you do what he tells you to do. And you say something the way he tells you to say it. The reason I don't want to live and entangle myself with a lot of people... living like a bee in a beehive... and that's how it would be there.

Linda Corley, Ph.D.

Mrs. Marcel: All I want is the money. (Laughter) I'll baby sit with the pets. I told him I'd bank the money any time he'd send it back. But you know, I think if he'd go over there [Hollywood]... It's hard when you have to memorize and remember... that's a lot. He did so well out there [interview at his home's back yard] though. He sat there and whenever they'd say stop and start again... He [director] said, "Remember exactly where you stopped." Whose to say he can't do that again? I think that's it.

Jesse: Well, I had to narrate 32 years of experience. In quick sequence. And every time the wind would make a little noise the roof...

Mrs. Marcel: Yeah, they'd have to stop.

Jesse: They'd stop that thing and put another number in and clap that thing and then bam.

Mrs. Marcel: You know those things they crack?

Linda: They really do those things, don't they?

Jesse: Oh, do they!

INTERNATIONAL GROUP ONE

Linda: This [film footage] is not Johnny Mann's stuff?

Jesse: No, no. That was filmed by International Group One. That group from Los Angeles that called me. The telephone rang here at ten o'clock one morning. In 1979 they called me. I answered the telephone at ten o'clock.

Linda: The book [*The Roswell Incident*] didn't come out till 1980.

Jesse: Well, no. The book doesn't cover that.

For The Sake of My Country

Linda: But what did they know about you in 1979?

Jesse: From Stanton Friedman. He's the guy who called me here. Anyway, they sent this troop out here of four people. They had the sound man, the camera man, the technical director, and the director. They left Los Angeles... right when they boarded the plane, they called me at ten o'clock which was eight o'clock their time. And at six o'clock that evening they were right here. It was non-stop from Los Angeles to New Orleans. They got a big station wagon and loaded up all their equipment and at six o'clock that evening they all pulled up here.

Linda: And you repeated all of that [Roswell events] to them?

Jesse: Well, that evening, that first evening, we're out there in the living room. I wanted to find out what they wanted. And we went over papers and papers and papers. And the director told me what he wanted me to do. I said, "OK, I'll try." He said, "Tomorrow morning at ten o'clock we'll set up our camera equipment right here on the porch. And your going to sit there and we'll film you." They filmed from ten o'clock that morning... with just little breaks... till six o'clock that night. I was sitting there narrating. He said, "Narrate everything you kept secret," that I could remember from 32 years back.

Linda: You didn't tell me half of that stuff you must have said to them. But I've already got it in the book [*The Roswell Incident*].

Jesse: Yeah, it's in the book. You see, what's in the book there, was taken from that narration for the film. That was International Group One. They exposed, good gosh, I don't know how many roles of 16 mm film.

Linda: So, you must be tired repeating that story, huh?

Jesse: Yeah. (Laughter)

[I was not interested in Jesse repeating his story as he had previously told it. This information was hashed over on TV all week and in the

Linda Corley, Ph.D.

recent book The Roswell Incident, so I stayed away from those details. I wanted something more, either an exclusive, or something about him personally. That is what I got.]

Linda: You're sick of it, huh? Well, we had more fun. We didn't do the "story" we just talked. That's more fun than repeating the story, huh?

Jesse: Yeah, that's far better. I've enjoyed this afternoon. Cause every now and then I can come out and tell you something you didn't know.

Linda: Yeah, I know. And it's more about you and your feelings, too. See, I believe that... I don't know if these people who have interviewed you before actually believe. I believe [in the existence of UFOs].

TELEPHONE INTERVIEWS

Jesse: Linda, one day I got a call from New York City. WRCA radio in New York City calling. I had to give them a telephone interview on my telephone. And I was on the air. They were on the air with me in New York City. Same thing with KTRS TV in Houston. Same way.

Linda: And I'm sitting in your kitchen. (Laughter)

Mrs. Marcel: Yeah, but they didn't even tell him he was on the air.

Jesse: Not at the time I was [on the air], no. They said at the conclusion, yeah. WGN called me. They wanted to send a camera crew over here.

Linda: So, you've had only one camera crew here?

Mrs. Marcel: Oh, no.

Jesse: No, three [camera crews]. Two from Los Angeles. You see, I'm popular. (Laughter)

Linda: I know that. I got your autograph somewhere over here. [Referring to his signature on the drawing he did earlier.] If I can get that man from Pascagoula... if I can find him [Calvin Parker]... and believe me Golden Meadow [Louisiana] is not big enough to hide him. If I ask him would he consider to talk about it to you...

Jesse: I'd be glad to talk to him. You better cut this thing [recorder] off.

Linda: I have almost 3 full tapes.

END OF INTERVIEW

ANCIENT WRITING

DEMOTIC HIEROGLYPHS

Mrs. Marcel told me that she was the first one to describe the symbols on the beams found at the debris field as some sort of Egyptian writing but without pictures of animals, as usually seen in Egyptian writing. I explained to the Marcels that I had seen such writing before, and the next day showed them a picture of ancient writing called Demotic Hieroglyphs. They both agreed that this was very similar to what they saw.

A sample of Demotic Hieroglyphs can be seen on the Rosetta Stone located in the British Museum in London. On the Rosetta Stone are two languages, Greek and Egyptian. The Egyptian portion is written in two forms: Hieroglyphic and Demotic. The Demotic text is the middle group. A Frenchman, Jean Francois Champollion, labored for 15 years on the decipherment. His work became the foundation for all the later progress by Egyptologists in the study of hieroglyphs.

While man's creative and destructive powers have been developing for an incalculable number of years, the intellectual progress of mankind developed only at a very late stage; only yesterday, a few thousand years ago, can it be said that man's spiritual advance

Linda Corley, Ph.D.

began. It is very important from the point of view of the history of writing, to stress the significance of this fact.

By about 3000BC, the Egyptians had worked out a system of writing called hieroglyphic. The word comes from the Greek hieros, "sacred," and glyphe, "carving." The ancient Egyptians attributed the creation of writing to Thoth, the god who invented nearly all the cultural elements. The Babylonian god of writing, Nebo was also the god of man's destiny. Greek myths attributed writing to the god Hermes. The ancient Chinese, Indians, and many other peoples also believed in the "divine" origin of script. Some believe that esoteric knowledge from the past foretells the future and releases secret powers. All very interesting concepts.

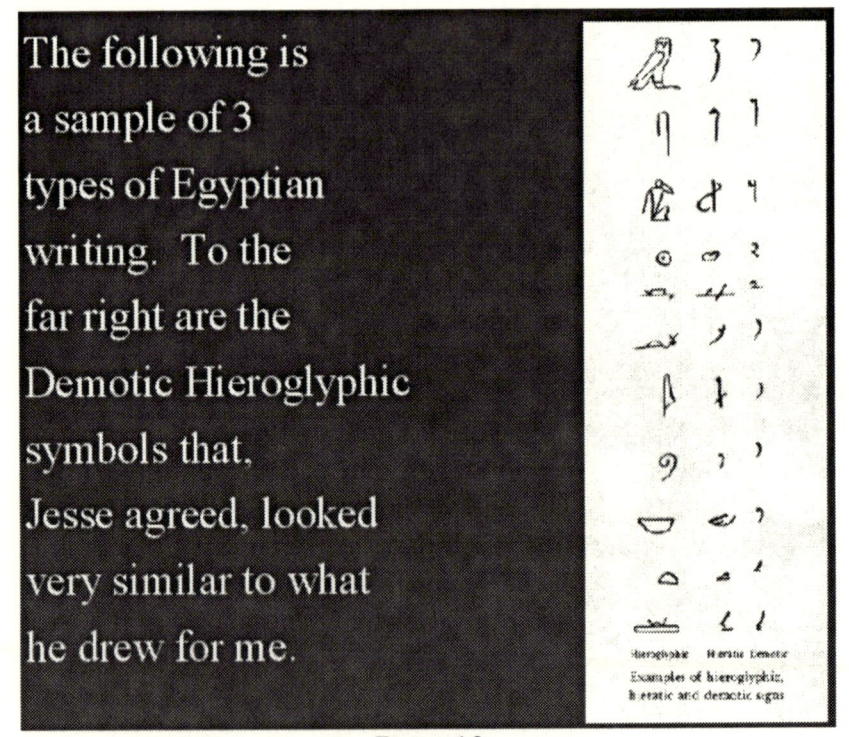

The following is a sample of 3 types of Egyptian writing. To the far right are the Demotic Hieroglyphic symbols that, Jesse agreed, looked very similar to what he drew for me.

Figure 10

The above symbols were given to Jesse the day after the interview. I was able to translate a few of the symbols. The Demotic Hieroglyph for **"there"** (1st symbol from the top), the Hieroglyph for **"his"** (6th

118

symbol from the top), the Hieroglyph for **"truth"** (7th symbol from top), the Hieroglyph for **"it"** (8th symbol from the top), and the Demotic Hieroglyph for **"lord"** (the 9th symbol from the top) are the ones that appear similar to the 6 symbols Jesse drew for me. It was extremely difficult to find other Demotic Hieroglyphs in order to make a comparison of the other Marcel symbols. However, with a little more research, I later found a similar writing dating back to 63 BC. This writing was not as old as Demotic writing which dated back to 700BC.

TIRONIAN NOTES

The oldest form of shorthand that we know from antiquity is the so-called Acropolis System of the Greeks of the Fourth Century BC. Amongst the Romans, a true shorthand is due to Cicero's secretary Marcus Tullius Tiro (circa 100 BC). The collections of such signs, up to 13,000 handed down to us date from only the eighth to tenth centuries AD. The system of the Tironian Notes consists in that the basic signs stand for a whole word.

This writing remained in use for about 1000 years, until the Latin language had changed radically and secret writing had become associated with witchcraft. Ancient manuscripts, as are written in the Tironian shorthand, remained undecipherable until 1747, when the French scholar Charpentier succeeded in reading them and published an account of them. (Another Frenchman)

The third line, center block, contains the script which closely resembles what Jesse drew for me. With further research into Latin translations I came across some very interesting translations.

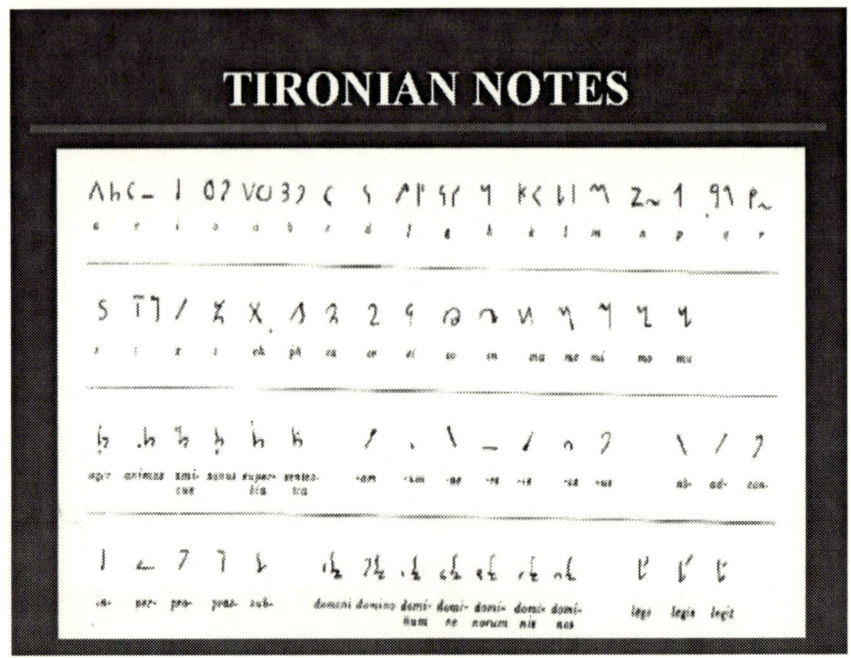

Linda Corley, Ph.D.

Figure 11

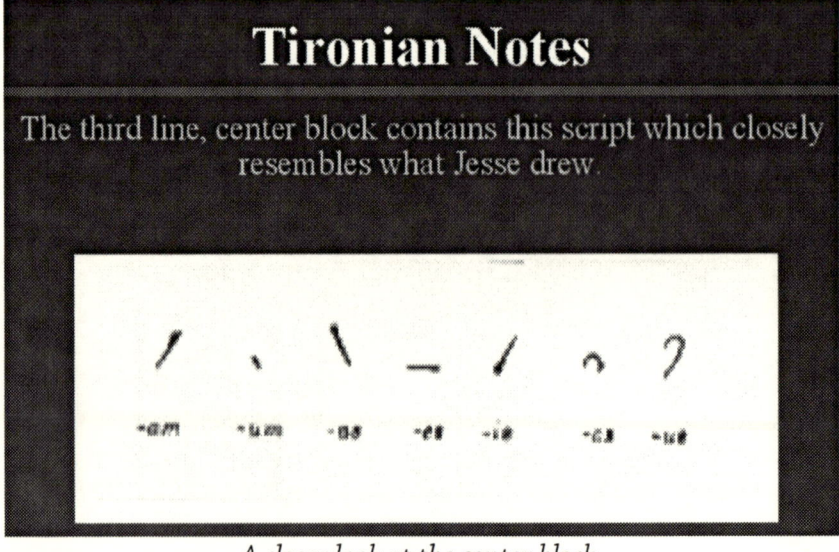

Tironian Notes

The third line, center block contains this script which closely resembles what Jesse drew.

A closer look at the center block.
Figure 12

120

It appears that Jesse's 6 symbols are similar to all of the above symbols except for the second one. Notice in Figure 10 the symbols at the end of the third line. The first two of these 3 symbols also appear similar to Jesse's symbols.

I attempted to translate all 10 of these symbols using their Latin word meanings (**am, um, as, es, is, os, us, ab, ad, con**) and found 8 translations. Here is what I found using a Latin translator for ancient text.

1. am--round/around
2. um-- forefathers, ancestors.
3. as--unity
   1. **as** , assis, m. , old form **assarius** , ii, m.;
   2. in general, *unity, a unit*.
   3. *round slice*
4. **es--to be/ exist/live/take place/happen/occur**
   1. consume, devour; destroy
5. is--to go/sail/fly/move
   1. **is** , ea, id
   2. go, walk; march, advance; pass; flow; pass (time); ride; sail;
   3. *he, she, it; this* or *that* man, woman, thing.
   4. referring to something already mentioned, in general.
   5. referring to the *third person*:
6. os--the mouth
   1. **os** , oris
   2. *gen. plur., n., the mouth*
   3. mouth, speech, expression; face; pronunciation; os, ossis bone; (implement, gnawed, dead); kernel (nut); heartwood (tree); stone (fruit); os, ossuis bones (pl.); (dead people);
7. us--provisions, supplies, victuals
   1. **us** , i, f., = Mallos, *an inhabitant of Mallus*, **Mallus** or **Mallos** was an ancient city of Cilicia Campestris lying near the mouth of the Pyramus (now the Ceyhan Nehri) river, in Anatolia. In ancient times, the city was situated at the mouth of the Pyramus, on a hill opposite Magarsus which served as its port. The location of the site is currently inland a few km from the

Mediterranean coast on an elevation in the Karatas Peninsula, Adana Province, Turkey, a few km from the city of Karatas.

8. **ab--until/in time and other relations in which the idea of departure from some point/to designate separation or distance/from a point of time/to take or carry away from some place**

   1. **ab,** antithesis to *ad* (as in to *go forward*)
   2. **ab** PREP by (agent), from (departure, cause, remote origin/time);

9. **ad--to/toward/first/the point or goal at which any thing arrives/nearness or proximity**

   1. **ad** , prep. with acc. - from the fourth century after Christ written also **at.**
   2. In a progressive order of relation, **ad** denotes, first, the direction toward an object; then the reaching of or attaining to it; and finally, the being at or near it.
   4. Direction toward, *to, toward*, and first, in space.
   5. The point or goal at which any thing arrives.
   6. **ad** ADV about (with numerals); ad PREP ACC ad PREP ACC to, up to, towards; near, at; until, on, by; almost; according to.

10. con--to learn by heart, without book

More specifically, Jesse's 6 symbols appear to closely resemble the Latin words and their translations that I have highlighted in bold above. Using the order in which Jesse wrote, the symbols read as follows: **is, ab, ad, es, os, us.** Just for the fun of it, let's see what this loosely translates into.

"To go sail, fly, move - from a point in time to take or carry away from some place - toward first the point or goal at which any thing arrives - to be, exist, live, take place, happen and occur - the mouth speech - provisions from Mallos."

The symbols Jesse drew for me have always been my main interest, out of all the Roswell events. I had long had an interest in ancient writing and secret codes and scripts. So you can imagine how I felt when Jesse gave me this drawing of what he believed was alien writing.

I have taken the liberty to draw various beams of Jesse's drawing to further enjoy his description of the beam. To quote him, "They [the symbols] were pink and purple. The main character might be pink and the tone behind it was purple. The others were purple... and switched around."

Below are several versions I have developed for **my own enjoyment**.

ENJOY!

Linda Corley, Ph.D.

Figure 13

Figure 14

Figure 15

THE END
(OR IS IT?)

FINAL THOUGHTS

In my interview with Jesse Marcel, Sr. one of the things I wanted to know was if a paradigm shift had taken place in his reality as a result of the incident at Roswell. Looking back, I think it did.

As far back as 1947, he believed that there were other intelligent beings in the universe and that there was a government conspiracy to prevent the public from learning more about the UFO phenomenon. He believed that there was a technology that could run circles around any technology that we had. He may have assisted the government in their denial of the existence of these paranormal events, for many years, but in the end he came forward and told the public what he knew.

Jesse left this physical world and I'd like to think that he has traveled to that strange hyper-reality from which the Extraterrestrials seem to emerge. I expect to see him there.

To quote the editors of Fortean Times, "In this vague and complex data-wilderness there can be no experts, only people who honestly want to find knowledge and understanding. The business of 'finding out' is bound to offend most - those with closed minds or who have a vested interest in the status quo."

VISITED CHILDREN

As we journey into the 21st century our awareness of the significance of UFO sightings and intelligent life visiting this planet, enhances our desire to function in this world at a higher level and to integrate mind, body, and spirit so to improve the quality of life for ourselves and those traveling with us. Because this is a universe of unlimited possibilities, why limit ourselves? The time is indeed at hand to leave our fear behind us and don a fresh garment of celestial brightness for the new life we are destined to live as divine "**visited children**" in the third millennium. It is my hope that the new millennium will bring us opportunity to discard the old ways of being and thinking, that may well have served us in the past, but will no longer help us in the future. I would like to end with these words of wisdom.

A Recognition of Unity

*I recognize a vital unity
linking me with all humanity
and humanity with all life,
acknowledging that where
none prevails over another,
each may prosper
and all may continue.*

BIBLIOGRAPHY

Berlitz, Charles, & Moore, William L. 1980. *The Roswell Incident*. NY: Berkley Books.
Bowman, Alan & Thomas, David. 1983. *Vindolanda: the Latin writing tablets*. London: Society for the Promotion of Roman Studies, pp. 71-72.
Carpentier, 1747. *Alphabetum Tironianum*, Paris.
Chatelain. Paris, 1900. *Introduction a la Lectures des Notae Tironiennes*.
Claiborne, Robert. 1974. *The Birth of Writing*. NY: Time Life Books.
Costamagna, G., Baroni, M.F., Zagni, L. 1983. Notae Tironianae quae in lexicis et in chartis reperiuntur novo discrimine ordinatae. Fonti e studi del corpus Membranarum Italicarum, Ser.2, Fonti Medievali 10. Rome.
Diringer, David. 1968. *The Alphabet: A Key to the History of Mankind*. NY: Funk & Wagnalls.
Ganz, David. 1990. *On the history of Tironian notes*, in P.F.Ganz (ed. 1990): 35-51.
Ganz, David. 1990. *Tironishe Noten*. King's College London, On the History of Tironian Notes, Wiesbadden.
Jensen, Hans. 1969. *Sign, Symbol and Script*. NY: G. P. Putnam's Sons.
Kopp, *Ulrich Friedrich. 1817. Palaeographica Critica*, vol. i; Becker, *Gallus,* vol. i pp197, 198.
Mentz, A. 1944. Die tironischen Noten. Berlin.
Mertz, Barbara. 1964. *Temples, Tombs and Hieroglyphs*. NY: Dodd,

Mead & Co.

Scott, Joseph and Lenore. 1968. *Egyptian Hieroglyphs For Everyone*. NY: Funk & Wagnalls Publishing Co. Inc.

Tufts University. 2006. *Perseus Project*. Latin Translator, *Perseus Lookup Tool*, Internet Website- http://www.perseus.tufts.edu/cgi-bin/vor?lang=la

University of British Columbia Mathematics Department, Latin Dictionary, Internet Website- http://www.sunsite.ubc.ca/LatinDictionary

University of Notre Dame. 2006. Latin Translator, Latin Dictionary and Grammar Aid. Internet Website- http://www.nd.edu/~archives/latin.htm

Words by William Whitaker. 2006. Latin Dictionary and Grammar Aid. Internet Website - http://www.nd.edu/~archives/latin.htm

For The Sake Of My Country

Part Two

Added Commentary 2002

By

Linda G. Corley

TABLE OF CONTENTS

TABLE OF FIGURES — 137
PREFACE — 139

CHAPTER ONE
INTELLECTUAL PROGRESS OF MANKIND — 141
    WRITING'S DEVELOPMENTAL STAGES — 141
    THE FIRST WRITTEN LANGUAGE — 143
    EGYPTIAN HIEROGLYPHS — 147
    A BRIEF LOOK AT HISTORY — 150
    MODERN EGYPT — 151
    DISCOVERING THE KEY — 152
    THE ROSETTA STONE — 154
    STIMULUS DIFFUSION — 156

CHAPTER TWO
SECRET WRITING — 158
    A THEORY OF MY OWN — 158
    CRYPTOLOGY — 162
    TRANSFORMED WRITING — 163
    SUBSTITUTION WRITING — 163
    BREAKING ENEMY CODES — 164
    ESPIONAGE AND CRYPTOGRAPHY — 165
    EXTRATERRESTRIAL WRITING — 166

CHAPTER THREE
SOLVING THE MYSTERY — 169
    INTELLIGENCE ON OTHER WORLDS — 169
    GODLIKE ASTRONAUTS — 171
    ORIGIN OF INTELLIGENCE — 174

CHAPTER FOUR
THE PLANETARY SOCIETY — 178
    TODAY'S SPACE PROGRAM — 178
    COSMOGONY — 181
    COSMIC PURPOSE — 182
    PANSPERMIA — 184

ARE WE ALONE?	**185**
WORMHOLE COSMONAUT	**188**
DIRECT CONFRONTATION	**192**
PARADIGM SHIFT	**193**
WORLD VIEW	**195**
FINAL THOUGHTS	**197**
BIBLIOGRAPHY	**199**

TABLE OF FIGURES

1.	Figure 1 Demotic Hieroglyphs	148
2.	Figure 2 Tironian Notes Middle Block	159
3.	Figure 3 Tironian Notes	160
4.	Figure 4 Oannes	173
5.	Figure 5 Wormhole In Space	188
6.	Figure 6 Shortcut Through Space	189

PREFACE

On September 26, 1999, I spoke at the National UFO Conference (NUFOC) in San Antonio, Texas. This was the first time that I had presented the information that I obtained from my 1981 meeting with Lt. Col. Jesse A. Marcel, Sr. I had put together some highlights from the manuscript that I was working on as well as some slides of the beam and symbols Jesse drew for me. It appeared that the presentation was well accepted and I was flanked by many curious individuals after my talk. What surprised me the most was the fact that these individuals wanted to know more about the symbols on the beam and not about Jesse himself. There was nothing I could say to these people as I had not gone any further with my research into ancient codes and script. I was satisfied that I had found a similar writing and thought that it would make for interesting reading.

However, when I returned to Louisiana from my trip, I decided to delve a little more into the history of script and attempted to decipher the symbols that Jesse had drawn for me. I planned to present my findings at my next speaking engagement.

On July 15, 2000, I spoke at the 2000 MUFON International Symposium in St. Louis, Missouri. My presentation was titled, "For The Sake Of My Country - An Intimate Conversation With Lt. Col. Jesse A. Marcel, Senior." The material presented at the Symposium was taken from a 69-page manuscript I had transcribed from nearly four hours of audio tape of my conversation with Jesse and his wife in May of 1981. The manuscript was also available for purchase, for the first time. It included my own interpretation of the symbols Jesse drew for me.

My presentation and question and answer period lasted for one hour and appeared to be well received. Once off of the podium, and for the following three hours, I answered questions posed by conference attendees about the symbols and my interpretation of them. This seemed to be what held the most interest. I gave out my business cards and e-mail address for those interested in purchasing my manuscript as well as keeping in touch with me.

Since that time, I have had many inquiries from interested individuals concerning my opinion of the material Jesse gave to me during our visit; including the information about the Roswell incident as well as the drawing of a beam and symbols he remembered seeing while handling the debris he picked up at the crash site in Roswell, New Mexico.

I have put off giving my opinion on many issues, mainly due to the fact that I am not as well read on the subject of UFOs and Roswell as I might need to be if I were going to have to answer questions on the subject. Since my appearance in St. Louis, I have attempted to familiarize myself with many different theories. I have the good fortune of living only one hour from the Louisiana State Director's MUFON office and travel there monthly in order to check out videos and books on various topics in UFOlogy from the MUFON library.

Having now exposed myself to many theories, I have developed my own concepts concerning the visitors and all of the experiences that go along with sightings. These added four chapters will act as an addendum to my six chapters from the manuscript of my meeting with Jesse in 1981.

CHAPTER ONE
INTELLECTUAL PROGRESS OF MANKIND

> There is hardly any aspect of our present culture and civilization whose roots and precursors cannot be found in Sumer.
>
> -- ZECHARIA SITCHIN

WRITING'S DEVELOPMENTAL STAGES

My intense interest in the writing found on the craft beam Jesse Marcel Sr. described to me eventually led my research to the study of ancient writing. In order to lay the groundwork for the following chapters, it is critical for us to take a brief look at the developmental stages of writing.

While man's creative and destructive powers have been developing for an incalculable number of years, the intellectual progress of mankind developed only at a very late stage; only yesterday, a few thousand years ago, can it be said that man's spiritual advance began. It is very important from the point of view of the history of writing, to stress the significance of this fact (Diringer, 1968).

Some would say that among all the revolutionary creations of man, writing ranks as the supreme intellectual achievement. It was invented not once but perhaps as many as six separate times, in places as distant from one another as China and Central America.

Linda Corley, Ph.D.

Each effort began with simple pictures and plain strokes or dots - adequate for recording objects and numbers (Claiborne, 1974).

The Sumerians, thought to be the first inventors of writing, inhabited southern Mesopotamia in the Fourth Millennium B.C., in the region now occupied by Iraq. Their earliest script appears in the archeological record around 3100 B.C.

Their script evolved into the system of wedge-shaped marks called cuneiform. Meanwhile, hieroglyphic writing - the combination of pictures and signs that remains one of the most exquisite and complex scripts ever devised - was being developed to meet the needs of Egypt's royalty and priesthood, nearly a thousand miles away.

Sometime around 2500 B.C., writing was invented for the third time by the Elamites, whose territories lay in an area now occupied by Iran, about 200 miles east of Sumer. The Elamite script is puzzling to scholars, who have not yet succeeded in deciphering more than a few fragments. How the script came into existence and what course of development it followed also remains a puzzle. In any case, the inhabitants of Elam later discarded their own script and took over cuneiform, adapting the Sumerian signs to the phonetics of their own language. In the same period, writing was invented yet again by the civilization centering in the Indus Valley, in present-day Pakistan.

Soon after 2000 B.C. writing was invented for the fifth time, in the maritime kingdom of Crete. Bt 100 B.C. another invention of writing had appeared in Asia Minor - a script called Hittite hieroglyphs, though the forms of the characters bear no resemblance to those of Egyptian hieroglyphs. At about the same time, writing was invented again, far to the east, in the valley of the Yellow River in China.

The climax of writing's developmental stage came near the end of the Second Millennium B.C. with the emergence of the Phoenician alphabet - precursor of the printed script of the book you are holding in your hands. The alphabet led to the complex uses of writing we know today, and inevitably to their technological offspring, from the printing press to the high-speed computer printout.

However, even today, the story of writing and its beginnings is far from completely told. Ancient writing systems discovered in Crete and Mexico and Pakistan remains largely impenetrable. And the decipherment of important cuneiform records, such as those of the Sumerians, has not automatically revealed the meanings of others; for instance, the Elamite script used by early settlers in Iran has not yet yielded its secret.

Like many a tool - and many a talisman - writing was invented in many places, often independently. Over a period of more than 2,000 years - roughly from 3000 to 1000 B.C. - it arose in more than half a dozen societies.

The difficulties involved in an investigation of this enormous field of human knowledge demands a new type of historian. A historian who is like an anthropologist, ethnologist, psychologist, classical scholar, archaeologist, or Egyptologist (Diringer, 1968).

THE FIRST WRITTEN LANGUAGE

The first revolution in human communication occurred when the Sumerians - and shortly thereafter the Egyptians - developed written languages. Slightly older than the Egyptian civilization was that of the Tigris-Euphrates Valley, where writing was developed by the Sumerians shortly before 3000 B.C. This was the first system of writing anywhere in the world, and from that moment, history begins, since it meant that events could be recorded (Asimov, 1982).

This step had stupendous impact. With writing, humans could record their deeds and transactions, give lasting form to their thoughts and visions, and preserve their laws and commandments.

Linda Corley, Ph.D.

Writing proved a mighty thrust to progress and vastly speeded the growth and spread of civilization (Constable, 1987).

The Sumerian system of writing went through several developmental stages, a number of them roughly paralleled by the Egyptian. The first stage in Sumerian writing was clearly pictorial, with picture-symbols standing for concrete objects and actions. A stylized drawing of a human head meant "head"; two wavy lines meant "water."

But quite soon this limited system was extended by making certain pictures stand for less easily communicated words. The Sumerian sign for "mouth" also came to mean "speak." In a short time, the system was expanded again by the combination of symbols. A literate Sumerian of about 2800 B.C. knew that the linked signs for "mouth" and "food" meant the verb "to eat."

Scholars have considered the epic tales of the Sumerians and assert that 5,500 years ago they were the founders of the world's first high civilization, in what is today the Middle East. One theory contends that highly advanced aliens brought the human race into existence some 300,000 years ago. Many millennia later, in ancient Sumer, they passed on the gift of civilization (Flaherty, 1992.).

The early Sumerians called the aliens Anunnaki, or "those who from heaven to earth came." They revered the celestial visitors as gods, for from them the Sumerians had learned how to live. According to the ancient texts, wisdom was given by the aliens around 3760 B.C. This gift of knowledge included everything from medical prescriptions to calculations with numbers. At the same time, the gods, as Earthlings considered them, conferred the tradition of monarchy upon the Sumerians and taught them to create an organized society based upon the concept of universal justice.

When the Sumerians appeared in southern Mesopotamia (present day Iraq) in the middle of the fourth millennium B.C., life changed dramatically. It was as though humankind abruptly grew up. No one knows for sure where the Sumerians came from, because their language and culture have no traceable antecedents, but they did things that no human beings had done before. They irrigated their farmlands, built magnificent structures, conceived a complex religious faith, practiced law and medicine, and used written language. Scholars call this eruption of civilization "astonishing" and "extraordinary." It appears that the Sumerians were able to march off the arduous path of social evolution and spring far ahead because they had guidance and direction from the Anunnaki.

According to Zecharia Sitchin (1980), who has done extensive research in Sumerian texts, it was in Sumer that all the essential elements of a high civilization suddenly blossomed out, as though from nowhere and for no apparent reason. There is hardly any aspect of our present culture and civilization whose roots and precursors cannot be found in Sumer: cities, high-rise buildings, streets, marketplaces, granaries, wharves, schools, temples; metallurgy, medicine, surgery, textile making, gourmet foods, agriculture, irrigation; the use of bricks, the invention of the kiln; the first-ever wheel, carts; ships and navigation; international trade; weights and measures; kingship, laws, courts, juries; writing and recordkeeping; music, musical notes, musical instruments, dance and acrobatics; domestic animals and zoos; warfare, artisanship, as well as prostitution. And above all, the knowledge and study of the heavens, and the gods, "who from the Heavens to Earth had come."

Let it be clarified here that the Sumerians did not call these visitors to Earth gods. It is through later paganism that the notion of divine beings or gods has filtered into our language and thinking. The Sumerians called them DIN.GER, "the Righteous Ones of the Rocketships."

From the Sumerian cosmological tales and epic poems, from texts that served as autobiographies of these gods, from lists of their functions and relationships and cities, from chronologies and histories called King Lists, and a wealth of other texts, inscriptions and drawings, we have pieced together a cohesive drama of what had happened in prehistoric times, and how it all began.

It was from the twelfth member of the solar system, the Sumerians said, that astronauts had come to Earth - the "Gods of Heaven and Earth." It was from such Sumerian beliefs, that all the other ancient peoples acquired their religions and gods. These gods, the Sumerians said, created mankind and eventually gave it civilization - all knowledge, all sciences, including an incredible level of a sophisticated astronomy.

It was some 450,000 years ago, the Sumerian texts claim, that astronauts came to earth in search of gold. Not for jewelry, but for some pressing need affecting survival on the Twelfth Planet.

The first landing party numbered 50 astronauts; they were called Anunnaki - "Those of Heaven Who Are on Earth." More Anunnaki were landed on Earth, until their number reached 600. It was not long before the young Anunnaki, short of female company of their own, took to having sex with the daughters of Man. Since they were all of the same first Seed of Life, and Man was a hybrid created with the genetic "essence" of the Anunnaki, the male astronauts and the female Earthlings discovered that they were biologically compatible; "and children were born unto them." The original purpose of coming to Earth, the sense of mission, the dedication to the task - were dissipated and gone. The good life seemed to be the main concern of the Anunnaki.

Under the Amorite domination, the Sumerians finally broke and declined rapidly, losing their identity, though their culture remained to be inherited and elaborated by conqueror after conqueror. The language died out as a living vehicle for communication but remained as part of religious liturgy (like Latin in the modern Catholic Church) for some 1500 years, not dying out completely till 300 B.C. (Asimov, 1968).

As the functions of many of the written symbols changed, so did their appearance. The formal Egyptian hieroglyphs, suitable for incision on stone monuments and temples, gave birth to a less pictorial script called hieratic, which was better suited to writing with ink on paper like papyrus. The simple pictographs that early

Sumerian scribes had scratched in their clay tablets became highly stylized characters (Constable, 1987).

Humans had found a way to make permanent their perishable thoughts, to carry them across space to distant places and across time to all succeeding generations. Many cultures would evolve their own scripts in the centuries to come, but the next revolution in communications, the invention of printing, would not take place for almost 5,000 years.

EGYPTIAN HIEROGLYPHS

Along with other major developments of Egyptian civilization came writing. By about 3000 B.C., the Egyptians had worked out a system of writing called hieroglyphic. The word comes from the Greek hieros, "sacred," and glyphe, "carving." There were more than 600 hieroglyphic signs, used mainly by priests for religious inscriptions and other formal writings.

The ancient Egyptians attributed the creation of writing to Thoth, the god who invented nearly all the cultural elements, or to Isis. The Babylonian god of writing, Nebo was also the god of man's destiny. An ancient Jewish tradition considered Moses as the inventor of script. Greek myths attributed writing to Hermes or to other gods. The ancient Chinese, Indians and many other peoples also believed in the divine origin of script (Diringer, 1968).

Hieroglyphs were a combination of ideograms and phonograms. The Egyptians did not develop a true alphabet, but they did progress toward one. They had twenty-four signs with only one letter each - all consonants. They had some eighty signs containing two consonants. There were no signs for vowels (Constable, 1987).

The Egyptians gradually simplified hieroglyphic writing. An even simpler script was called demotic. Throughout their history,

Linda Corley, Ph.D.

however, the Egyptians continued to use hieroglyphs to carve official records on public buildings.

Egyptian pictorial writing is one of the most attractive systems of writing ever devised. Incidentally, the correct noun form for the little images is "hieroglyphs." Popular writers occasionally call them hieroglyphics, and this small error scratches at the sensitivity of Egyptologists like a fingernail on a blackboard. The hieroglyphic (adjective) script is of course quite distinct from the Egyptian language.

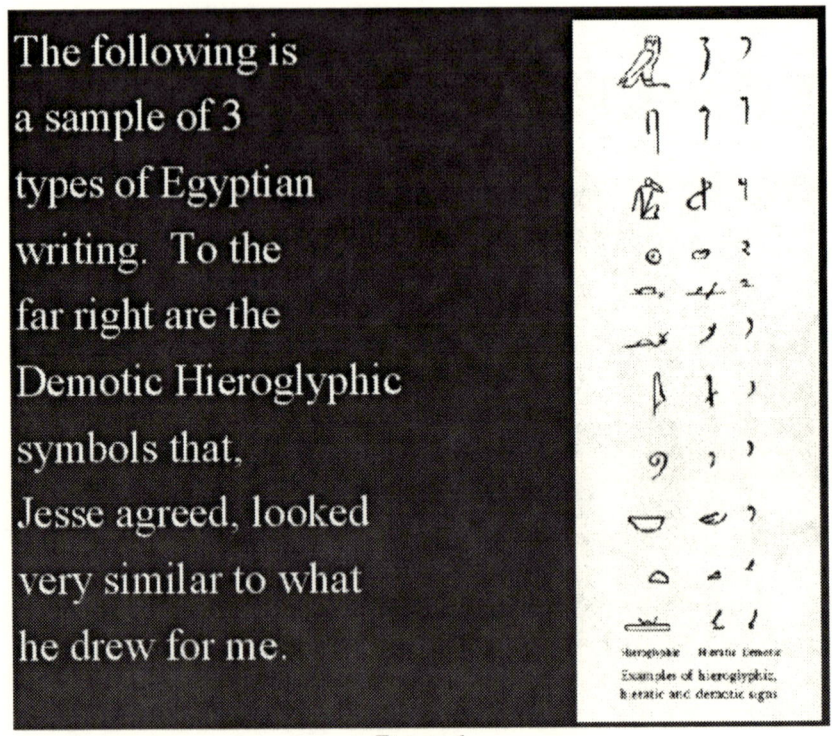

The following is a sample of 3 types of Egyptian writing. To the far right are the Demotic Hieroglyphic symbols that, Jesse agreed, looked very similar to what he drew for me.

Figure 1
Demotic Hieroglyphic Symbols

Various forms of the Egyptian language are written in hieroglyphic script. They were written in another script as well - the "shorthand" form known as hieratic. Over the years the forms became more and more cursive, until eventually the hieratic signs bore only a distant resemblance to their hieroglyphic ancestors. The hieratic was written with a pen, on papyrus, but even this script was too tedious for the overworked scribes of the later bureaucracy.

Although hieratic was a simplified form of writing the hieroglyphs in script form, a more rapid style of writing began to predominate around 700 B.C. This was the "demotic" style, derived from the Greek word "demotikos," or popular. It continued in use until about 500 A.D. (Scott, 1968). (See Figure 1)

This was after Tutankhamon and Ramses and before Alexander the Great and Cleopatra. A sample can be seen on the Rosetta Stone located in the British Museum in London.

Hieratic writing is child's play compared to demotic. At its worst, demotic consists of row upon row of agitated commas, each of which represents a totally different sign. It is perfectly dreadful stuff to read.

Demotic emerged as a new form of writing, mainly because the hieratic business hand had deteriorated so much that it had become obscure. Thus demotic, the new more cursive form of hieratic, having developed in lower Egypt into a proper system of writing, became gradually the "popular" script of the whole of Egypt. It was used at first for ordinary purposes such as business and private letters but, in course of time, it was employed also for lengthy literary compositions and for copies of ancient books. In time demotic gradually developed; it received its stereotyped form about 300 B.C. On the whole, demotic is very difficult to read, and the main difficulty lies not in the language, but in the script. Demotic continued to be used until the very end of Egyptian paganism in the fifth century A.D. Moreover, it handed on to the Coptic alphabet certain signs, for sounds which could not be expressed by Greek letters (Diringer, 1968).

In the Egyptian language, there were drastic changes even with Pharaonic Egypt, in addition to later alterations. Major forms of the written language are identified as old Egyptian (Dynasties 1 through 10), Middle Egyptian (Dynasties 11 through 18), Late

Egyptian (Dynasties 19 to 25), Demotic (Dynasties 26 to the beginning of the Christian era), and Coptic (from Christianity until Islam's influence).

Coptic language and script developed after 300 A.D. as the mode of expression by the Christian descendants of the ancient Egyptians. It is still used in some church services today, although little understood (Scott, 1968).

After the Arab conquest, Coptic was gradually replaced by Arabic. By 1500 A.D. it was virtually extinct, although its use lingered in small outlying areas and in isolated groups descended from the native Egyptians.

Coptic was written in the Greek alphabet, supplemented by seven characters based on demotic writing to write sounds occurring in Egyptian but not in Greek. The language is a very late stage of Egyptian, different in many ways from the older tongue of the early periods.

A BRIEF LOOK AT HISTORY

Egypt is an alluring concept. One moment it is a far-off country with an impressive array of antiquities, a tantalizingly-lucid style of art and a vaguely-sensed sweep of history; the next it is an obsession. Travelers swear that nowhere else is like it. Some believe that esoteric knowledge from the past foretells the future and releases secret powers. And beware, for anyone can succumb (Evans, 1979).

The Greek historian Herodotus, who traveled through Egypt around 450 B.C., wrote a lengthy account of what he saw and learned, the earliest record from outside Egypt. He confessed his enthusiasm for things Egyptian: "No other land possesses so many wonders, nor has such a number of works that defy description." Herodotus saw the country when pharaohs still occupied the throne and when the temples still had priests who claimed to know their history. He enjoyed a good story and happily wrote down anything they told him.

After Herodotus and the Greeks came Julius Caesar and the Romans. Caesar conquered Egypt, established the heiress-queen Cleopatra (actually the seventh Cleopatra) firmly on the throne and may have fathered her son, Ptolemy Caesar. After Caesar's death, Marc Antony married Cleopatra.

Christianity came to Egypt as early as the first century but, for a hundred years and more, Christians were harshly persecuted. Eventually, in A.D. 313, Constantine the Great made Christianity one of the recognized religions of Rome. The Bible was soon translated into Coptic, the language spoken by Egyptians.

After Christianity came Islam. In the seventh century an army of sixteen thousand sweeping in from Syria wrenched Egypt from the grasp of the Roman empire. Alexandria fell to the Arabs in A.D. 641.

MODERN EGYPT

The greatest event in modern Egypt was the arrival of Napoleon Bonaparte in 1798. He had managed to persuade the Directory in Paris that this would be the best way of destroying British influence in the Mediterranean and recovering India, which, like Alexander before him, worked powerfully on his imagination. The importance of the occasion was not so much military as scholarly. With him he took scientists of all kinds, geologists, botanists, historians, engineers, and surveyors, with the idea of recording and assessing the resources of the country. It was a remarkably farsighted thing to do. Having defeated the Mamelukes at the Battle of the Pyramids - after making his famous utterance about four thousand years of history looking down on his army, which, if it was a guess, was a peculiarly informed one because it anticipated scholarly opinion by quite a few years - Napoleon established himself in Cairo at the "Institut d'Egypte," which published many great volumes in Paris between 1809 and 1828 (Newby, 1989).

One of the people in Napoleon's train was the engineer Bouchard, to whom fell the honor of discovery of the hieroglyphs by Champollion. This laid the basis for the modern study of Egyptology.

On July 1, 1798, Napoleon invaded Egypt. Although he quickly secured the country, after landing near Alexandria, the expedition became a strategic and political fiasco. Napoleon fled back to France in August 1799 (Evans, 1979).

Napoleon had originally taken with him a Commission of Arts and Science, a party of scholars, scientists and artists charged with the task of investigating every aspect of contemporary Egypt and its antiquities. During their three years in Egypt the Commission carried through an incredible amount of work; sketching, measuring, and collecting. They eventually published the results of their researches, beginning in 1809, in twenty-four large and lavishly illustrated volumes.

Most important of all, the expedition happened to discover the key to the deepest mystery of ancient Egypt; the meaning of the hieroglyphs. Everyone concerned with Egypt accepted that the hieroglyphs would prove significant, although, as yet, they had no way of translating them. Completely by accident, some of Napoleon's soldiers stumbled across the clue that would make all the difference (Constable, 1987).

DISCOVERING THE KEY

A detachment of soldiers working on some fortifications near Rosetta in the western Delta happened to turn up a slab of basalt, a fine-grained black stone, over 3 feet high, somewhat less broad and about 1 foot deep. The soldiers noticed that the face carried inscriptions and sent the stone, the Rosetta Stone, to the members of the Commission in Cairo. Their excitement stemmed from the fact that the inscription came in three bands. The topmost, half broken away, consisted of fourteen lines of hieroglyphs; the middle had thirty-two lines of demotic script, a simplified form of Egyptian writing; the bottom section, fifty-four lines of it, was in Greek. They could translate the Greek. It recorded a decree of the Egyptian priesthood in 196 B.C. and this gave them hope of deciphering the hieroglyphic version (Evans, 1979).

Even with this key, finding the solution took a further twenty years and involved a number of scholars sifting through many more inscriptions than just that on the Rosetta Stone. Some of them mislead themselves by clinging to the idea that hieroglyphs had to be symbolic and purely a picture language. Others handicapped themselves by refusing to admit any link with Coptic, the later language of Egypt. Others, still, went so far with their researches and then drifted off to take up other interests. One man in particular pulled together everything that was known about hieroglyphs.

Jean Francois Champollion was born in Figeac in the southeast of France in 1790. By the time he was eleven years old he had decided that he would be the decipherer of hieroglyphic writing. He was eighteen years old when he began his work on the Rosetta Stone (Constable, 1987).

Champollion obtained reproductions of every available Egyptian text and, over a fifteen-year period, compiled from them all the forms of the hieroglyphic signs, with their simplified hieratic and demotic equivalents. He set himself to learn all the languages that might be useful, including Coptic, before, at age of eighteen, he turned to the Rosetta Stone. He started with the demotic inscription. In 1822 he was able to publish "A Letter Regarding the Alphabet of the Phonetic Hieroglyphs." Champollion went on correcting and extending his ideas until his death in 1832. By then, he had made an expedition to Egypt and prepared a dictionary and grammar of Ancient Egyptian. His work has been the basis of all subsequent study of hieroglyphs (Evans, 1979).

Linda Corley, Ph.D.

Hieroglyphic writing mixed together different ways of representing words. Some of the signs really were pictures. The pictures of a face meant a face; an eye was an eye; a circle with a dot at the center was the sun. Some, although still pictorial, expressed more abstract concepts so that the picture of a scepter implied the idea of ruling. These picture signs could also stand for the letters of the word they represented.

In writing hieroglyphs, the Egyptians usually worked from right to left or top to bottom, although they could set them out from left to right or in other patterns if necessary. They turned the signs around so that they always faced the beginning of the message.

THE ROSETTA STONE

The Rosetta Stone is three feet nine inches high, two feet four and a half inches wide, and eleven inches thick. It is but part of a larger piece, estimated to have been five or six feet high originally. The missing parts have never been found. The Rosetta Stone itself ended up in the British Museum, as spoils of war (Scott, 1968).

On the Rosetta Stone are two languages, Greek and Egyptian. The Egyptian portion is written in two forms: Hieroglyphic and Demotic. The Hieroglyphic text is topmost of the writings. This writing style was used throughout Egyptian history for nearly all documents and monuments intended for public viewing where the mantle of formal presentation was desirable. The Demotic text is the middle group, being highly abbreviated "handwritten" form of the hieroglyphs. Actually, this was the principal and popular writing form of the time when the stone was carved. The Greek text is the language shown at the bottom. Therefore the implication of the writing was that the stone was carved after the arrival of Alexander the Great in 332 B.C.

When copies of the Rosetta Stone texts reached Europe, scholars went to work on it immediately. The Greek text was translated by 1802. Results from the first studies of the Demotic portion were achieved the same year by Akerblad, a Swedish diplomat. He identified all of the proper names in the Demotic section which occurred in the Greek section, plus a few other words. All of these were written alphabetically. Brilliant as was his work, it led him to the assumption that the rest of the Demotic was alphabetic. This was to prove in error, but it would take 12 years before the erroneous premise was set aside. The mistaken assumption also existed that some of the signs were vowels, which caused other false starts.

It was not until 1814 that the scientist Thomas Young deduced that the Demotic writing was not entirely alphabetic. By 1816 he had developed a vocabulary of 86 words associating the Greek with the Demotic. He then found that the groups of hieroglyphs with ovals around them, or cartouches as they are better known, contain royal names. Using several hieroglyphic texts, he recognized the names of Cleopatra and Berenice, and that of Ptolemy.

This breakthrough by Young helped pave the way for the work of Jean Francois Champollion, who had been laboring independently on the decipherment and was coming to similar conclusions. By the time he had reached the year of his death in 1832, Champollion had corrected and greatly enlarged Young's list of hieroglyphs, and deciphered the names and titles of most of the Roman emperors who had ruled Egypt. He also formulated a system for understanding the Egyptian grammar and evolved a method of decipherment which became the foundation for all the later progress by Egyptologists in the study of hieroglyphs.

The first section of the Rosetta Stone says that in the ninth year of the reign of Ptolemy V, Epiphanes by name, a decree was passed by the General Council of Egyptian priests. They were meeting at Memphis to commemorate the anniversary of the coronation of Ptolemy V as king of all Egypt. The year was 196 B.C. The stone notes the occasion, first giving the date, and then publishing a series of epithets which proclaimed the devotion of the king to the gods, and his love for the Egyptians (Constable, 1987).

The second section of the inscription on the Rosetta Stone listed 17 benefits that Pharaoh Ptolemy V had conferred on Egypt. Included were gifts to the temples, forgiveness of debts, the release of prisoners, reduction of taxes, the sending of troops against Egypt's enemies, and restoration of sacred buildings (Scott, 1968).

In gratitude, according to the stone, the priests decided to put statues of Ptolemy in every temple, create a new holiday for him, and make shrines to him to be loaned to private individuals for their homes and for carrying in processions. It was also ordered that copies of the decree be set up in "all temples of the first, second, and third orders." That is why one copy of the decree was found at Rosetta, and other copies of the text have since been found at different locations in Egypt.

STIMULUS DIFFUSION

How did civilization arise in Egypt? Was it independent creation? The American anthropologist A. L. Kroeber has suggested the term "stimulus diffusion" to cover a type of borrowing from other civilizations. A people may borrow the idea of doing something from another culture, but the way in which it is done may be their own way. The Egyptians did not copy Sumerian writing. All they needed was the great idea that the spoken word could be recorded. Obviously the borrowing culture must have reached a stage of development in which the new concept is understood and desired (Mertz, 1978). Some experts argue that Egypt seems to have borrowed the new idea but substituted native forms for foreign symbols. This theory is very difficult to prove (Diringer, 1968).

Not all scholars accept "stimulus diffusion" as the explanation for how civilization arose in Egypt. Some of them believe in a "dynastic race" who entered Egypt at the end of the prehistoric period, bringing with them the gifts of civilization. They unified the land and ruled the conquered indigenes as a racially distinct noble class, before interbreeding and contact produced a single people. The dynastic race came from Asia. They spoke a Semitic language, which mingled with the Hamitic (African) tongue of the natives to produce the Egyptian speech. One cannot summarize the conflicting theories of origin more precisely than that (Mertz, 1978).

There has been a fascination with Egypt, for many people, in years past. Sometimes an interest in Egypt showed up in odd places. Every country that could grabbed an obelisk. Italy already had several, shipped there by the Roman emperors. Augustus used one as a giant sun dial and calendar. Another had found its way to Istanbul. One, lifted by Giovanni Belzoni from the Temple of Philae, graced the grounds of a private house in Dorset, England. In the 1830s, the French took one of Ramesses II's obelisks from the Temple of Luxor and set it in the Place de la Concorde, Paris. The Romans had shifted a pair of Tuthmosis III's obelisks from Heliopolis to Alexandria. In 1878 the British took one to London, placing it beside the River Thames and Christening it "Cleopatra's Needle. The Americans made away with the other in 1880, moving it to New York City's Central Park (Evans, 1979).

Whatever culture pushed civilization to arise, Egypt has had the longest unbroken cultural span in history - 3,000 years. Knowledge in this part of the world preceded that of today by 3,000 to 5,000 years in many realms of mathematics, astronomy, agriculture, political science, domestic science, medicine, literature, defense, philosophy, ceramics, pottery, and art (Scott, 1968).

CHAPTER TWO
SECRET WRITING

> Egypt was the first civilization in recorded history to use aspects of cryptology in writing.
> -- Fred Wrixon

A THEORY OF MY OWN

My interest in Egypt and its written language is the basis of my theory of the writings on the craft beam that Jesse Marcel drew for me. In the many hours of research on Egyptian writing, I was eventually convinced that the drawing Jesse drew for me looked exactly like Demotic Hieroglyphs. While preparing the Marcel manuscript, I realized that it had been a long time since I read a book on ancient languages. This was all put aside over 20 years before. However, my decision to publish the Marcel tapes led me back to the research of man's first steps toward writing.

So back to the library I went and in a book on signs, symbols, and script I found a picture of writing that dated back to 100 B.C. This writing was not as old as the Demotic writing which dated back to 700 B.C. The writing was a form of shorthand and looked amazingly like Jesse's drawing. This was a magnificent discovery for me. As my excitement grew, I searched the library shelves frantically for other representations of this writing. What I found will astound you. It is a picture of writing that was represented in several sections of script and known as the Tironian Notes.

For The Sake of My Country

Tironian Notes

The third line, center block contains this script which closely resembles what Jesse drew.

/ , \ — / ∩ ?

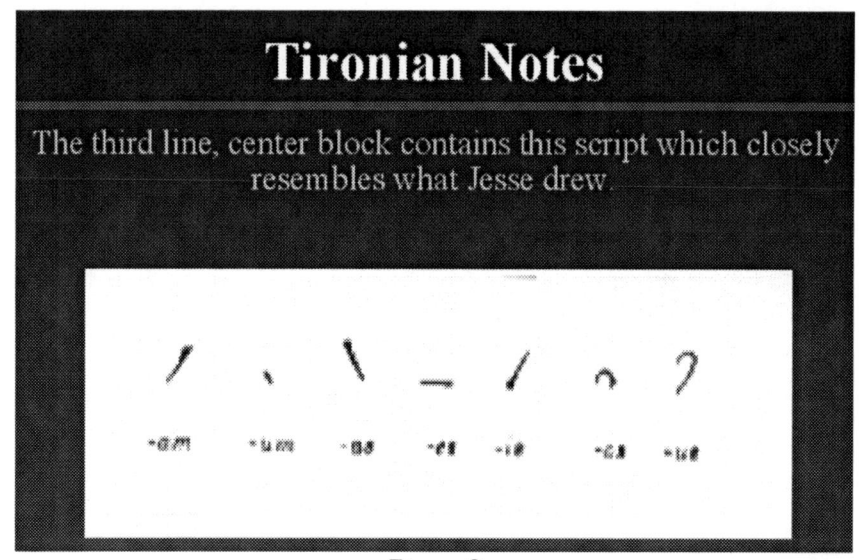

-am -um -as -ei -ie -ca -ue

Figure 2
Tironian Notes

There are five declensions of nouns in the Latin language. The first declension (-a, -ae, -ae, -am, -a, -ae, -arum, -is, -as, -is) is primarily made up of feminine nouns, but some naughty masculine ones have snuck into it. Most Latin students use the acronyms PAINTS (Poeta, Agricola, Incola, Nauta, Tata, Scriba) or APPIAN (Agricola, Poeta, Pirata, Incola, Auriga, Nauta) to remember the most frequently used masculine nouns in the first declension (Internet Site: 1999: geocities.com/Athens/Forum/6946/masculine).

One section of this script, except for the inversion of two symbols, eerily resembled what Jesse drew for me. (See Figure 2)

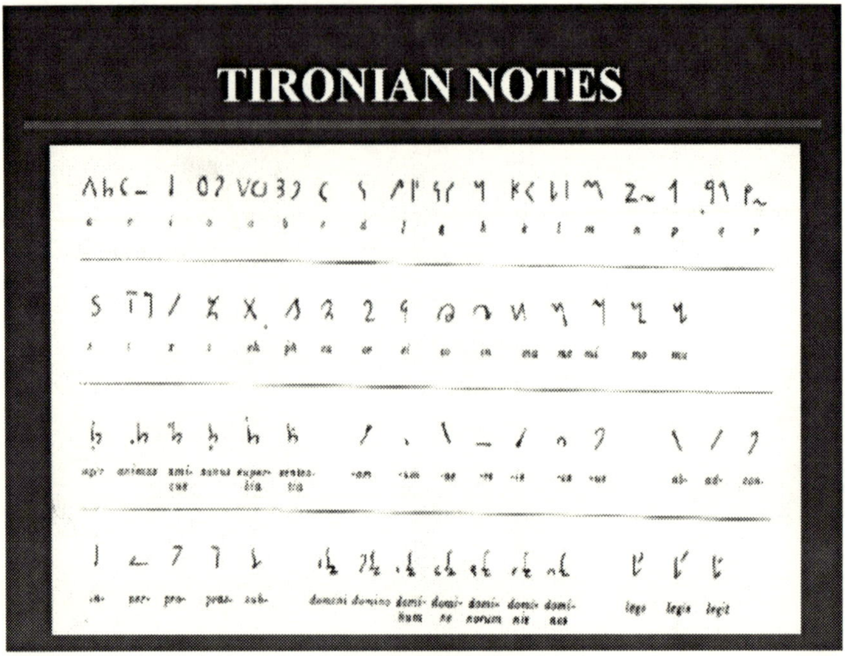

Linda Corley, Ph.D.

TIRONIAN NOTES

Figure 3
Tironian Notes

To give the reader some background on these symbols, the oldest form of shorthand that we know from antiquity is the so-called Acropolis System of the Greeks which is handed down to us from the acropolis in Athens of the fourth century B.C. Another attempt to achieve abbreviation meets us on the fragmentary Delphic Consonant Tablets found at Delphi (Jensen, 1969).

Amongst the Romans, the poet Ennius (239-169 B.C.) Is supposed to have been the first to create so-called "notae vulgares," that is to say, probably word abbreviations in which the usual letters were retained. A true Roman shorthand, in the sense of an abridgement of the normal script-signs, is due to Cicero's secretary Marcus Tullius Tiro (circa 100 B.C.). He himself created abbreviations for the most frequent words, above all for the prepositions, and these were further increased by his pupils. The collections of such signs - up to 13,000 - handed down to us date from only the eighth to tenth centuries A.D. The system of the so-called "Tironian Notes" consists in that the basic signs are either the letters of the capital script or of the majuscule cursive or also abbreviations of these. Now a basic sign, by assuming a somewhat modified form or position, stands for a whole word. Compounds of several basic signs also serve the same purpose.

While Tiro probably wrote only the stems of words and suppressed their endings or wrote them out in full, his successors invented a means of further shortening, by adding the endings through dots, dashes and so on in certain positions. The development of the Tironian Notes proper was completed for the time being by Seneca (died A.D. 65). The commentary written by him contains about 5,000 abbreviated signs.

In a hypothetical terrestrial situation, if I wanted to write information in a secret code so no one could readily decipher it, would I use a 2,000 year-old shorthand script? I'll admit that this sounds like a problem that only the X-Files and Agent Mulder could solve. However, I ask myself if this theory is fitting.

Could the writings have been done by terrestrials who knew that it would be almost impossible to decipher ancient script? Could the craft have been a top secret project of some government? Do governments have a secret language all their own?

It is quite evident that governments throughout the world have used codes and ciphers for centuries. How plausible is it, in our hypothetical "terrestrial scenario," that the government responsible for the debris picked up at Roswell also used a code and cipher or secret language on their secret air craft?

Linda Corley, Ph.D.

CRYPTOLOGY

News reports and headlines are often dominated by accounts of espionage, spy rings, and suspected traitors. Sharing the newsprint and camera lights are reports of arms-control debates, weapons like the stealth bomber, and futuristic space research. These subjects are connected to each other in terms of military and national security interests. Sometimes such issues seem vague and too complex for most of us to understand, but they fascinate us nonetheless (Wrixon, 1989).

Cinematic and real-life spies are expected to send concealed messages. Diplomats have special phrases for embassy and personal use. Concealment methods are intended to deny access by a third party (i.e., "the enemy") to the contents.

Cryptology is the science that includes making messages secret (cryptography) and solving of those messages by those meant to have them or by third parties, the "opponents," who are not meant to have them. Cryptologists use codes and ciphers.

A code is a method of concealment that may use words, numbers, or syllables to replace the original words and/or phrases of a message. One specific way that codes differ from ciphers is by the substitution of whole words as contrasted with the letters that are substituted or transposed in ciphers. A cipher is a means of concealing a message. The letters of the message are substituted or transposed for other letters, letter pairs, and sometimes for many letters.

While codes were the prime choice for masking communications in the past, ciphers have been predominant since the early 1900s. Ciphers have proved to be better adapted than codes in the modern electronic age because of the easy application of their two main forms: transposition and substitution.

TRANSFORMED WRITING

Transposition is a system of cryptography whereby the letters of a message are rearranged. Generally, it is a less complicated method than substitution, which is a system of cryptography whereby the letters of a message are replaced by other figures, numbers, or letters.

Egypt, an advanced early civilization, was the first in recorded history to use aspects of cryptology in writing. Early Egyptian hieroglyphs contained some figures that were somewhat altered from their original form. Though not a code or cipher by any means, this change did involve a basic principle of cryptology, namely, that of transforming writing (Wrixon, 1989).

As the Egyptian civilization expanded, hieroglyphics became more involved. This writing was used primarily to describe religious texts and rituals. In a desire to protect these texts and impart teachings with added respect, priests had scribes make still more changes. When special figures were created for these specific purposes, secrecy, another central principle of cryptology, became involved. The religious hierarchy took advantage of its powers of "translation" for the increasingly less informed, and thus more dependent, people.

Secret writing, with codes and ciphers, is almost as old as writing itself. History is full of the stories of kingdoms, armies, and people that have been destroyed by that fatal disease. Again and again, the story has been the same: the secret writing was not secret enough. Some enemy puzzled out the method, and was able to uncover the secret (Moore & Waller, 1962).

SUBSTITUTION WRITING

Julius Caesar is a man who affected history in a number of well-documented ways including his style of hidden writing. Most people are not aware that he communicated with ciphers. While he was building the Roman Empire in Gaul, he communicated with a substitution type that still bears his name today (Wrixon, 1989).

In the Caesar Cipher the plaintext letters were substituted for letters three steps along a natural alphabet progression. Thus if Caesar had been using English, "f" would have aligned with "i." Julius Caesar lived in the era of Rome's ascent to glory. But like other nations before her, Rome entered stages of decadence and decline. When the Roman Empire finally crumbled, chaos reigned. The fragile lights of education as well as cryptology were nearly extinguished when the Dark Ages swept over much of the known world.

BREAKING ENEMY CODES

In more recent times, during World War I, the American Government built up an effective organization for breaking enemy codes and ciphers and eventually cracked the Japanese secret-writing systems (Moore & Waller, 1962).

In the growing tension of the prewar years from 1933 to 1941, the United States quietly reestablished an organization to break the codes and ciphers of potential enemies. This outfit was known as the National Security Agency. Insiders will tell you that the initials "NSA" stand for "Never Say Anything." In World War II, our code-crackers identified themselves by the code name MAGIC.

With the advances in science and industry, a vast array of equipment once imagined only in science fiction is at play. The reality of jet planes, nuclear submarines, intercontinental ballistic missiles, and computers are making technology the focus of concern (Wrixon, 1989).

In the 1960s America was making quantum leaps in so many areas that the Soviets and others began to fear a "facts gap" and reacted accordingly. A new era of industrial spying evolved and gave birth to a different breed of sellout specialist, the technological traitor.

One of the advanced technological systems that can be applied to codes, ciphers, and secret languages is the computer. Computers have subsets of common tongues called programming languages. This is necessary because standard verbal usages are often ambiguous in definition and application. However, the real benefit to the secret message maker comes in the expansive options available for creating codes and ciphers. A vast world opens up with millions of possibilities to confuse even a skilled cryptanalyst. Thus, the cipher solvers have to arm themselves with their own versions of these marvels.

By the 1960s technology was given the highest priority among the cloak-and-dagger set. America's industrial centers were assigned the special target emphasis that the KGB had once applied to the atomic Manhattan Project.

ESPIONAGE AND CRYPTOGRAPHY

On May 20, 1985, retired United States Navy warrant officer John Walker was arrested by the FBI on suspicion of espionage. This complex and tragic story exemplifies the crucial importance of protecting encrypted technology. As a navy radioman, John Walker used a KL-47, an electronic rotor machine. The KL-47 was a modern version of the types of cylinder devices that had developed from Thomas Jefferson's day and improved upon the rotors of World War II. This updated rotor mechanism was at the center of naval communications. The KGB wanted to break it so badly that they put some of their own best scientists to work on the mission.

The Soviets succeeded in providing Walker with a palm-sized, battery-operated device. It was a continuity tester that revealed the wiring pattern of the KL-47's rotors. The Russians used this knowledge to re-create the circuitry, then applied computers to seek the millions of possible encryption variations. When Walker also handed them real cipher/code key lists after his tours of duty, the navy's protection methods were completely undermined.

Technological treason is a great threat. It is not just the stuff of adventure movies or political science fiction. Every country has vital reasons for maintaining its own secure existence in an age where nuclear destruction is an electric impulse away.

EXTRATERRESTRIAL WRITING

Now let's go back to my earlier "terrestrial scenario." I will not waste my time or yours by entering into a discussion on the government's lame explanation of a Mogul Balloon. We will bypass that pitiful explanation in this book. However, I will entertain that the debris recovered in Roswell might have been part of a secret government project.

Of course I believe it is possible that our government covered up a military secret for all these years. A secret that consisted of our very own high-tech space craft with secret writing that no one could readily decipher. Why, of course that is a possibility. We had access to computers that could encrypt and decipher secret codes. Let us take a look at that technology of the 1940s.

In 1942, the theoretical physicist John V. Atanasoff and his assistant Clifford Berry built the first computer that successfully used vacuum tubes to do mathematical calculations. The machine was called the Atanasoff Berry Computer, or ABC (Berliner, 1990).

In 1946 the ENIAC - the Electronic Numerical Integrator and Calculator - was ready for operation. It was by far the most complex electronic device in the world. The ENIAC was not only the first fully electronic computer ever built but also just about the largest. It occupied roughly eighteen hundred square feet (Bernstein, 1963).

A large factor in the decision to build the ENIAC was military pressure. In the summer of 1944, the late Professor John von Neumann, who was then a consultant to the group engaged on the atomic bomb project at Los Alamos, started working in the field of electronic computing. His job at Los Alamos was to find techniques for performing the immensely involved numerical computations that were necessary in the design of nuclear weapons.

The ENIAC was the first electronic computer, that used vacuum tubes instead of relays and other semi-mechanical devices. The current in a tube's state involved stopping or starting the flow. In a vacuum tube, very strong electrical forces are brought to bear on the electrons, giving them very high accelerations in extremely short times, and the state of the tube could be changed in about a millionth of a second. If an electronic machine were to store its data in decimal, it would need ten vacuum tubes to represent the ten possible values for any one decimal place.

In the late 1940s, our government was so technologically advanced that they used a computer that contained 18,000 vacuum tubes which failed at the rate of one every seven minutes and cost a half a million dollars. That is really laughable. By today's standards, one pea-sized chip will deliver the same amount of computing power and any home computer costing a few hundred dollars could out perform that 50-year old technology. But this government built a secret space craft and used secret encrypted writing on it and when it was discovered would not lay claim to it. Now, wait a minute. Didn't I say that I believed out government might have been involved in whatever it was that crashed in Roswell in 1947? Hhuumm, let us try another theory.

Assuming the writings are indeed the Egyptian or Roman scripts I have mentioned, let's try this hypotheses. If the writings on the craft beams found by Jesse Marcel were not done by terrestrial government personnel but by extraterrestrial beings, then should we make the assumption that it came from another world? If it came from another world, could the writings have originally been given to the ancient Sumerians, Egyptians, or Romans by the extraterrestrial beings in order to advance the process of civilization? Or could the extraterrestrials have adopted the language and writings of the ancient peoples, in order to better communicate with them on Earth, on one of their visits to this planet over 3000 years ago? More fascinating hypotheses to ponder. Yet, a supposition on a very important communication link with another world.

There will surely be debate about these theories, however, I like them, so I am passing them on to you. Enjoy!

CHAPTER THREE
SOLVING THE MYSTERY

Since the remote past we have all lived in an evolutionary spiral that carries us irresistibly into the future, into a future which I am convinced has already been the past; not a human past, but the past of the "gods," which is at work in us and will become the present one day.

-- VON DANIKEN

INTELLIGENCE ON OTHER WORLDS

Since the dawn of history, man has speculated about the possibility that intelligent life may exist on other worlds beyond the Earth. Carl Sagan wrote that this idea probably originated from the often unsuccessful attempts of primitive religions to give meaning to those aspects of the environment which had no simple explanations (Shklovskii & Sagan, 1966).

As astronomy developed, the concept of the existence of life on other worlds began to acquire some scientific bases. Most of the early Greek philosophers, both the materialists and the idealists, thought that our Earth was not the sole dwelling place of intelligent life. Considering the limitations of science at the time, these early philosophers displayed great originality and ingenuity. Belief in the existence of extraterrestrial life continued to spread during the eighteenth and early nineteenth centuries.

Linda Corley, Ph.D.

The problem of life on other planets is no longer abstract. It has acquired practical meaning. Experimental methods are being designed for the direct investigation of our solar system. In 1966, Carl Sagan wrote about special devices for the detection of extraterrestrial life that will be landed on the surfaces of the planets and may provide a definitive answer to this age-old question. In 1997, the year of his death, such a device landed on Mars.

There is enormous public interest in the possibility of extraterrestrial life. Rapid progress is being made in the study of this problem. Sagan wrote that investigations of extraterrestrial intelligence are not scientifically superfluous and should not be relegated to the realm of fantasy and science fiction.

Are there other intelligences in the universe? Is the Galaxy filled with civilized worlds, diverse and unimaginable, each flourishing with its own commerce and culture, befitting its separate circumstances? Or can it be that we are alone in the universe, that by some poignant and unfathomable joke, ours is the only civilization extant?

The idea that we are not unique has proved to be one of the most fruitful of modern science. The atoms on Earth are the same in kind as those in a galaxy some 5 or 10 billion light years distant. The same interactions occur, the same laws of nature govern their motions.

One conceivable approach is to assume that civilizations in various stages of historical development exist throughout our Galaxy, and then to see what observational consequences this assumption implies. Humanity is relatively young; our civilization is in its infancy. Hominids have inhabited the Earth for about 0.1% of its history; our civilization has so far endured only for one-millionth the lifetime of the Earth; and technical civilization, in the sense of the capability for interstellar radio communication, has been present for about one-billionth of geological time. It is then immediately obvious that if there are civilizations on planets of other stars, they should, in general, be much more highly developed than our own.

Whether this development includes social, scientific, artistic, or technical aspects, or other aspects which we cannot even imagine, is difficult to foretell.

GODLIKE ASTRONAUTS

If ancient peoples experienced unusual occurrences described in their legends and myths about coming into contact with space voyagers, the astronauts would probably be portrayed as having godlike characteristics and possessing supernatural powers. Special emphasis would be placed on their arrival from the sky, and their subsequent departure back into the sky. These beings may have taught the inhabitants of the Earth useful arts and basic sciences, which would also be reflected in their legends and myths.

Carl Sagan wrote that once he came upon a legend which more nearly fulfills some of our criteria for a genuine contact myth. It is of special interest because it relates to the origin of Sumerian civilization. Sumer was an early - perhaps the first - civilization in the contemporary sense on the planet Earth. It was founded in the fourth millennium B.C. or earlier. We do not know where the Sumerians came from. Their language was strange; it had no cognates with any known Indo-European, Semitic, or other language.

The successors to the Sumerians were the Babylonians, Assyrians, and Persians. Thus the Sumerian civilization is in many respects the ancestor of our own. Sagan felt that if Sumerian civilization is depicted by the descendants of the Sumerians themselves to be of nonhuman origin, the relevant legends should be examined carefully. It is the type of legend that deserves more careful study.

Taken at face value, the legend suggests that contact occurred between human beings and a nonhuman civilization of immense powers on the shores of the Persian Gulf, perhaps near the site of the ancient Sumerian city of Eridu, and in the fourth millennium

B.C. or earlier. There are three different but cross-referenced accounts of the Apkallu (Sumerian givers of wisdom) dating from classical times. Each can be traced back to Berosus, a priest of Mel-Marduk, in the city of Babylon, at the time of Alexander the Great. Berosus, in turn, had access to cuneiform and pictographic records dating back several thousand years before his time. It is important to quote most of the body of the legend, in the form available today. The manner of presentation is as striking as the content. The quoted translations from the Greek and Latin are taken from Cory's Ancient Fragments, in the revised edition of 1876.

Here is the account of Alexander Polyhistor:

Berosus, in his first book concerning the history of Babylonia, informs us that he lived in the time of Alexander, the son of Philip. And he mentions that there were written accounts preserved at Babylon with the greatest care, comprehending a term of fifteen myriads of years. These writings contained a history of the heavens and the sea; of the birth of mankind; also of those who had sovereign rule; and of the actions achieved by them.

And, in the first place, he describes Babylonia as a country which lay between the Tigris and Euphrates. He mentions that it abounded with wheat, barley, ocrus, sesamum; and in the lakes were found the roots called gongae, which were good to be eaten, and were, in respect to nutriment, like barley. There were also palm trees and apples, and most kinds of fruits; fish, too, and birds; both those which are merely of flight, and those which take to the element of water.

In the first year there made its appearance, from a part of the Persian Gulf which bordered upon Babylonia, an animal endowed with reason, who was called Oannes. The whole body of the animal was like that of a fish; and had under a fish's head another head, and also feet below, similar to those of a man, subjoined to the fish's tail. His voice, too, and language was articulate and human; and a representation of him is preserved even to this day on an Assyrian cylinder seal of the ninth century B.C.

This Being, in the daytime used to converse with men; but took no food at that season; and he gave them an insight into letters, and sciences, and every kind of art. He taught them to construct houses, to found temples, to compile laws, and explained to them the principles of geometrical knowledge. He made them distinguish the seeds of the earth, and showed them how to collect fruits. In short, he instructed them in everything which could tend to soften manners and humanize mankind. From that time, so universal were his instructions, nothing material has been added by way of improvement. When the sun set it was the custom of this Being to plunge again into the sea, and abide all night in the deep; for he was amphibious.

Figure 4

The straightforward nature of this account of contact with superior beings is notable. Oannes and the other Apkallu are described variously as "animals endowed with reason," as "beings," and as "personages." They are never described as gods. Stories like this one and representations especially of the earliest civilizations on the Earth, deserve much more critical studies than have been performed heretofore, with the possibility of direct contact with an extraterrestrial civilization as one of many possible alternative interpretations.

There are also other possible sources of information. It seems possible that the Earth has been visited by various Galactic civilizations many times. It is not out of the question that artifacts of these visits still exist - or even that some kind of base is maintained within the solar system to provide continuity for successive expeditions.

The rate of technical advance of our civilization is very great. It is possible that an extraterrestrial society or federation or such societies might want to contact an emerging technical civilization as soon as possible, perhaps to head off a nuclear annihilation - one possible consequence of intensive technological development - or perhaps for other reasons.

ORIGIN OF INTELLIGENCE

Certainly the track of racial development to Homo Sapiens can be followed back clearly for millions of years, but we cannot make nearly so definite a statement about the origin of intelligence. In the course of the thousands of millions of years of general evolution, human intelligence seems to have appeared almost overnight. While still anthropoids, our ancestors created what we call human culture astonishingly quickly. But intelligence must have made a sudden appearance for this to happen (von Daniken, 1970).

Several million years passed before anthropoids came into being through natural mutations, but after that the Hominids underwent a lightning-like development. All of a sudden, tremendous advances appear about 40,000 years ago. The club was discovered as a weapon; the bow was invented for hunting; fire was used to serve man's own ends; stone wedges were used as tools; the first paintings appeared on the walls of caves. Yet 500,000 years lie between the first signs of a technical activity, pottery, and the first finds in hominid settlements.

Who was it that taught us to think? Anthropologist Loren Eiseley wrote that man emerged from the animal world over a period of millions of years and only slowly assumed human features. But there is one exception to this rule. To all appearances his brain ultimately underwent a rapid development and it was only then that man finally became distinguished from his other relatives.

The field of research devoted to the explanation of the origin of mankind is interesting and very worthwhile. Yet the question why, how, and from what date man became intelligent seems to be at least as interesting.

Eiseley believed that we must assume that man only emerged quite recently, because he appeared so explosively. He felt that we have every reason to believe that, without prejudice to the forces that must have shared in the training of the human brain, a stubborn and long-drawn-out battle for existence between several human groups could never have produced such high mental faculties as we find today among all peoples on the earth. Something else, some other educational factor, must have escaped the attention of the evolutionary theoreticians.

Is man a creation of extraterrestrial intelligence? There is a decisive factor that has not been taken into account in all the theorizing on the subject. Will we ever be able to supply the missing link without investigating the theory of visits to our planet by extraterrestrial intelligences and checking whether these beings should not be held responsible for the sudden appearance of intelligence? If there is life on other planets, did they bring with them to our earth branches of knowledge of the kind we are now acquiring? Did they make our ancestors intelligent?

According to the writings of von Daniken, the Sumerians had myths that told of "gods" who drove through the sky in barks and fire ships, descended from the stars, fertilized their ancestors, and then returned to the stars again. The Sumerian texts do not refer to their "gods" with vague imprecision; they say quite clearly that the people had once seen them with their own eyes. Their sages were convinced that they had known the "gods" who completed the work of instruction. We can read in Sumerian texts how everything happened. The gods gave them writing, they gave them instructions for making metal and taught them how to cultivate barely.

If they had indeed paid a visit to our planet thousands of terrestrial years ago, only a few decades would have passed for the crew of their spaceship. No eternities would have passed for the extraterrestrials since that visit to Earth.

Could cosmic memories have penetrated more and more strongly into our consciousness in the course of man's evolution? Did these memories encourage the birth of new ideas, which had already been realized in practice at the time of the visit by extraterrestrial intelligence? Is it possible that at certain fortunate moments the barriers separating us from the primitive memory fall? Then the driving forces brought to light again by the stored-up knowledge become active in us.

Did we receive knowledge and tools from ancient astronauts that enabled us to rise above the other creatures struggling for survival on earth? Are we creators or inheritors; descendant or beneficiaries of a civilization and culture transplanted to us from somewhere else?

It is only a coincidence that printing and clock making, that the car and the airplane, that the laws of gravity and the functioning of the genetic code, were invented and discovered almost simultaneously at different times in different parts of the world? Is it pure coincidence that the stimulating idea of visits to our planet by unknown intelligences has appeared simultaneously and been put forward in a great many books with completely different argument and sources? It is, of course, extremely convenient to dismiss ideas as coincidences when there seems to be no cut and dried explanation for them, but that is too easy a way out.

As we spiral into the future should we ask ourselves if this future has already been the past? It is the belief of von Daniken that this may not be a human past, but the past of extraterrestrial intelligence, which is at work in us and may become the present one day. It appears that some of us are still waiting for definite scientific proof. However, I believe WE are the definite scientific proof!

CHAPTER FOUR
THE PLANETARY SOCIETY

The universe is not static; every component from an electron to a galaxy is continually moving and such movement cannot proceed forever in the same direction. Sooner or later it must complete a circle, or stop and return in the opposite direction.
-- J. L. CLOUDSLY-THOMPSON

Alien astronauts may be travelers from the future, who have come back to present-day Earth in order to recapture their own past, and perhaps to change the course of history for the better.
-- MICHAEL SWORDS

TODAY'S SPACE PROGRAM

According to The Planetary Society, the U.S. space program stands at a crucial point. In the late 1990s, NASA Administrator Dan Goldin initiated a new and revitalized program of cheaper, faster, better, missions geared toward exploration. But continued, devastating budget cuts and efforts by special interests to protect their profits may torpedo new initiatives (Friedman, 1997).

On October 12, 1992, coinciding with the 500th anniversary of Columbus's landing in the New World, two giant antennas aimed into the cosmos were turned on in the most far-reaching exploration effort ever attempted. Launched at the Goldstone Station of NASA's Deep Space network in California's Mojave Desert, this was the start of NASA's hopeful Search for Extraterrestrial Intelligence, or SETI (Sullivan, 1993).

The space program has seen the cancellation or delay of new, scientifically vital missions. NASA's ambitious and promising SETI program was killed in its very first year. The long-anticipated Comet Rendezvous Asteroid Flyby was scrapped. Even the Cassini mission to Saturn was threatened, then scaled way back (Friedman, 1997).

A dramatic new plan for exploration, "Mars Together," and "Fire and Ice" mission to explore the Sun and Pluto, were approved by then Vice President Gore and Russian Prime Minister Chernomyrdin as joint projects between the two nations. Now both missions are threatened.

The Planetary Society was the inspiration of the late astronomer, Carl Sagan. Dr. Sagan spent his entire life enthralled by the wonders of the realms that lie beyond our own small, pale blue planet. He wanted others to experience the fascination and awe that he felt. He succeeded in this endeavor by reaching countless millions of people through his writing, speaking and teaching.

The Society has dedicated itself to continuing Dr. Sagan's leadership, inspiring humanity to explore new worlds and search for other life. With an international membership of over 100,000 people, the Planetary Society is the largest and most influential space interest group in the world.

Talking about space research is one thing, doing it is quite another. The Planetary Society is responsible for initiating numerous vital space exploration programs. For example:

* The Society initiated international testing of the high-risk but marvelously ambitious Mars Rover, ultimately launching a whole new push for telerobotic control.

* The Society, backed by the unwavering support of their members, operates the largest continuous SETI detection system on Earth. Their efforts include not only a radio telescope at Harvard, Massachusetts but a sister telescope near Buenos Aires, Argentina, conducting the only full-time search covering the skies in the Southern Hemisphere.

* The Society played a pivotal role with the French in developing and testing the Mars Balloon, an innovative means of sampling the Martian atmosphere and gathering low-altitude, high-resolution images from widely-spaced locations. More recently, they have helped test a second-generation version of the Mars Balloon.

* The Society organized the first international study for the exploration of Pluto, the last unvisited planet in our solar system. This project was being considered by NASA via the Pluto Express. The mission was canceled for budgetary reasons, but later replaced by the similar New Horizons mission which was successfully launched on January 19, 2006. It is expected to arrive at Pluto in 2015.

* The Society's funding for the Asteroid Discovery Project has helped locate potentially-destructive "near-Earth" asteroids. With mounting evidence that a massive asteroid wiped out the dinosaurs and that other devastating impacts could happen at any time it is vital that we know where they are and where they're heading.

To discover and explore new worlds, and to seek our counterparts in the depths of space, these are objectives of mythic proportions. Pursuing these endeavors for the benefit of the human species is a mark of The Planetary Society's dedication to a hopeful future.

COSMOGONY

Cosmogony is the study of the origin of the universe. According to Timothy Ferris, emeritus professor at the University of California at Berkeley, Cosmology is the science concerned with discerning the structure and composition of the universe as a whole. It combines astronomy, astrophysics, particle physics, and a variety of mathematical approaches including geometry and topology (Ferris, 1997).

Cosmology, once the province of mythology, is now a science. The task poses a marvelous challenge to the imagination of the cosmologists, whose charter to envision alternative universes is enlivened by the possibility that other universes may actually exist. In 1977 there were fewer than a hundred professional cosmologists in the world. Today there are more than a thousand.

By 1970 astronomers knew the approximate distances for about two thousand galaxies. By 1994 that figure had climbed to one hundred thousand galaxies and was going up fast.

One can ask what difference cosmology makes to our everyday lives. The answer to this question, oddly enough, is that it seems to matter a lot. For some reason, and nobody seems to know just why, virtually every human society, from ancient Egyptians to Native Americans to the residents of just about every towering city and tiny village today, has developed models for the universe and explanations of how it came into being. And these models influence our thinking in ways that are not always readily apparent.

The assumption shared by most cosmologists is that the universe is expanding from a big bang origin and has not merely contrived to make itself look that way. Here it is helpful to wield Occam's Razor, the dictum that the simpler of two otherwise comparable hypotheses is to be preferred.

William of Ockham was a rather radical empiricist. He is still famous for his principle of parsimony (simplicity), known as Ockham's Razor. Simply stated, this was his insistence that one should not prefer a more complicated explanation when a simpler one will do. For Ockham, less was more (Solomon & Higgins, 1996).

Ferris (1997) points out that as the twentieth century draws to a close, the big bang theory looks to be in pretty good shape. It is supported by several solid and more or less independent lines of evidence, and has at present no serious rivals. If one were asked to make a list of the greatest scientific accomplishments of the century, somewhere on that list - along with relativity and quantum theory, the elucidation of the DNA molecule, the eradication of smallpox and the suppression of polio, the discovery of digital computation, and many other worthy attainments - there would be a place for big bang cosmology.

COSMIC PURPOSE

Every monotheistic religion credits God with having created the universe. Timothy Ferris asks the question, "What can cosmology tell us about God?" Cosmology presents us neither the face of God, nor the handwriting of God, nor such thoughts as may occupy the mind of God (Ferris, 1997).

The larger the universe looms, the sillier it becomes to maintain that it was all put together for us. This makes it appear to be a lot of wasted space. To posit a human-centered purpose to the heavens smacks of a lamentable humorlessness about the human condition, as Bertrand Russell was quick to point out. "The believers in Cosmic Purpose make much of our supposed intelligence but their writings make one doubt it." Russell wrote, "If I were granted omnipotence, and millions of years to experiment in, I should not think Man much to boast of as the final result of all my efforts."

Atheists draw sustenance from cosmological findings indicating that the universe emerged from chaos. Evidence in their support is mounting. If the world emerged from chaos and works by chance, what role can there be for an omniscient creator? As the nineteenth-century English essayist Charles Bradlaugh wrote, "An atheist is certainly justified in saying the Bible God I deny; the Christian God I disbelieve in; but I am not rash enough to say there is not God as long as you tell me you are unprepared to define God to me." We would be better off if we left God out of cosmology altogether. The origin of the universe and of the constants of nature is a mystery, and may forever remain so. Whether atheist or believer, scientist or mystic, if we all seek to learn we are united in having not **a** faith but **faith** itself.

However, deep within the mystery there is the debate over evolution and natural selection. Darwin, Huxley, and others labored to show that in astronomy we no longer believe that an angel pushes each planet around the Sun; the inverse square law of gravitation and Newton's laws of motion suffice. But no one considers this a demonstration of the nonexistence of God. We are free to posit that God is responsible for the laws of Nature, and that the divine will is worked through secondary causes. In biology those causes would have to include mutation and natural selection. Many people would find it unsatisfying, though, to worship the law of gravity (Sagan & Druyan, 1992).

Carl Sagan wrote that evolution in no way implies atheism, although it is consistent with atheism. But evolution is clearly inconsistent with the literal truth of certain revered books, like the Bible.

Evolution suggests that if God exists, God is fond of secondary causes and factotum processes: getting the Universe going, establishing the laws of nature, and then retiring from the scene. A hands-on Executive seems to be absent; power has been delegated. Evolution suggests that God will not intervene, whether beseeched or not, to save us from ourselves. Evolution suggests we're on our own - that if there is a God, that God must be very far away. This is enough to explain much of the emotional anguish and alienation that evolution has worked. We long to believe that there's someone at the helm.

A principal means by which life evolves is by exploiting imperfections in copying despite the cost. Mutations have no plan, no direction behind them. Their randomness seems chilling. Progress, if any, is agonizingly slow. The process sacrifices all those beings who are now less fit to perform their life tasks because of the new mutation. It is not how we would do it. It does not seem to be how a Deity intent on special creation would do it.

We want to urge evolution to get to where it's going and stop the endless cruelties. But life doesn't know where it's going. It has no long-term plan. There's no end in mind. There's no mind to keep an end in mind.

PANSPERMIA

At the turn of the century, a remarkable proposal was advanced: that life came to earth from elsewhere. The father of this idea called it "Panspermia," and it channeled the debate over the origin of life into new directions. Svante August Arrhenius of Sweden was one of the first winners of the Nobel prize in chemistry. He proposed that spores of life are adrift throughout the universe (Sullivan, 1993).

This proposal was elaborated in 1954 by J. B. S. Haldane of Britain, who was one of the most unorthodox scientists of his time. He said that life itself may have had no origin. The universe may have had no beginning and life is coeternal with matter. He believed that life spores could be carried from one part of the universe to another by light pressure and that it was even possible that they were "launched into space by intelligent beings."

If you think this a preposterous act, here on Earth, a proposal by Carl Sagan was just as daring. Sagan proposed that we might send organisms to such lifeless planets as Venus. Conversely, it would be essential to ensure that the spores we dispatched did not land on a planet already inhabited, unleashing a catastrophic epidemic.

ARE WE ALONE?

Is life cosmically commonplace or rare? Is human intelligence a fluke or a spark of universal fire? Does our existence tell us anything about the universe?

The question of whether we are alone in the universe is ancient. What's new is that we are coming to possess tools that could give us a shot at answering it. Existing radio telescopes are capable of detecting signals transmitted by an alien civilization of comparable capacity anywhere in our quarter of the Milky Way galaxy (Ferris, 1997).

Frank Drake, in 1960, conducted the world's first SETI (Search for Extraterrestrial Intelligence) observations, training an 85-foot radio telescope at Green Bank, West Virginia, on two nearby sun-like stars and listening at a single frequency. Today, the SETI detection system includes a radio telescope at Harvard, Massachusetts and a sister telescope near Buenos Aires, Argentina, conducting the only full-time search covering the skies in the Southern Hemisphere (Friedman, 1997).

Should we expect visitors from another world, particularly after they have detected radio emissions revealing the emergence of intelligent life in our solar system? Shouldn't we look for evidence of earlier visitations?

Ferris points out that until a search turns up something, or an overwhelming amount of nothing, discussions of extraterrestrial life will remain largely speculative. One camp, composed mainly of astronomers and physicists, argues that extraterrestrial life is abundant. "I'm sure they're out there," declares the physicist Paul Horowitz, of Harvard, who runs a SETI search from a modest, 84-foot radio telescope equipped with receivers and analyzers which Horowitz and his students built largely by hand (Ferris, 1997).

The other camp, made up mostly of life scientists, maintains that while life may exist on other planets, the odds of there being extraterrestrial intelligence are so small that we are almost certainly alone in our galaxy, and perhaps in the entire observable universe. There are those that declare that SETI is a deplorable waste of taxpayers' money. However, the one publicly funded American SETI project was canceled and the remaining ones are all privately funded. Taxpayers' funds are no longer involved.

The pro-SETI argument goes like this. There are so many stars in our galaxy that even if only one percent of them are orbited by an Earth-like planet, that would still mean that there were more than a billion Earths in the galaxy. Life began promptly in the history of our planet - the earliest fossil cells date from within a few hundred million years of the formation of the earth's crust. This suggests that life arises readily - at least, on terrestrial planets blessed with liquid water - and therefore does not depend upon some sort of extraordinary luck. Once established, life is robust. Terrestrial life had survived numerous catastrophes that decimated living species, yet evolution proceeded quick.

Over the course of billions of years of evolution, intelligence will emerge, sooner or later, because it confers survival advantages on the species that possesses it, which is what evolution is all about. Where there is intelligence, soon there will be technology. Humans went from dugout canoes to spaceships in a scant fourteen thousand years. So it makes sense to use radio telescopes to listen for signals from other technological civilizations, as there are likely to be thousands of them in our galaxy.

The pessimists, to simplify their argument, reply as follows. First of all, Earth-like planets are probably much rarer than the optimists assume. The earth is unique in the solar system in that it's at just the right distance from the sun so that water, which we all agree is essential to life as we know it, exists here in all three states, as liquid, ice, and vapor. Were Earth's orbit slightly larger or smaller, this would not be the case, and life might very well not exist here. Even if we accept the hypothesis that there's lots of life in the galaxy, the optimists' reasoning collapses when it comes to the advent of intelligence. The optimists claim that intelligence confers a survival advantage on the species blessed with it, and therefore is selected for in the course of biological evolution. But if that is the case, why did intelligence not appear earlier in Earth's long history?

The optimists stand accused of inconsistency. They say that life is in the cards because it originated early in our planet's history but they also say that intelligence is in the cards, and it originated late. The error (if it is an error) springs from the discredited assumption that evolution is a stair step progression, a slow-grinding machine aimed at producing, eventually, human beings. It's not. Evolution is pointless and largely random, and the sequence of events that led to Homo Sapiens Sapiens is so long and tangled, so replete with chance events that might well have gone otherwise, that intelligence almost certainly has never appeared anywhere else in the universe. Such extraterrestrial intelligence as may exist might well be akin to that of whales, spiders, insects, and the millions of other species that have lived on Earth, gifted with quite enough acumen to conduct their own affairs but uninterested in building radio telescopes. Finding such life will be difficult, communication with it harder than with owl and earthworms here at home. So, the pessimists conclude, we're alone, and we might as well get used to it.

Does the evolutionary record testify that intelligence and the invention of science is a fluke? The ancient Greeks were superb philosophers, who in some sense set us on the road to science, but they produced virtually no technology and almost no real science of their own. As the anthropologist Loren Eiseley wrote, "Man, the self-fabricator, is so by reason of gifts he had no part in devising." We fail to understand not only how or why the gift was given us but, more to the point, why it keeps on giving - why our brains equip us for domination of our planet.

Did extraterrestrial intelligent beings visit this planet and give us the gift of intelligence, technology, and a glimpse into our future so that we may know their past when we arrive back where we started so long ago? T. S. Eliot (1943) wrote:

Linda Corley, Ph.D.

We shall not cease from exploration
And the end of all our exploring
Will be to arrive where we started
And know the place for the first time.

WORMHOLE COSMONAUT

Exactly how did the extraterrestrials visit this planet in their space craft with the ancient writings on them in order to give us intelligence and technology? There has been talk of black holes and wormholes and strings in space. Pick up a book on physics and you will find actual methods of space travel. Hhuumm, sounds like science fiction. I think I'll try to imagine from the point of view of a scientist. This is what they say.

Timothy Ferris (1997) explains that to envision wormholes, we must first borrow a traditional popular science image and portray cosmic space-time as a rubber sheet. The sheet is undulated, with depressions surrounding massive objects. Here and there we find infinitely deep depressions, bottomless. These bottomless pits represent black holes. Each has a fluted stem, like that of a vase meant to hold a single roe. Bend the rubber sheet so that the open, bottom ends of two such stems are joined together. The result is a wormhole - a tunnel connecting two distant points in space.

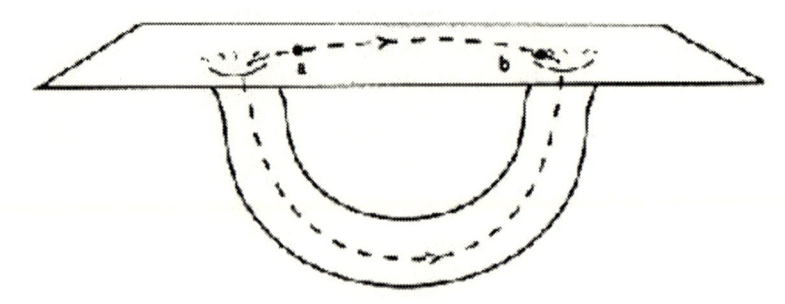

Figure 5
*Wormhole in space. Two points, **a** and **b**, may be connected by a path through "normal" space (dotted line) or one that threads through the wormhole (dashed line). The length of these two routes may be very different. As drawn, the wormhole path looks longer, but under some circumstances it can be much shorter, as depicted below.*

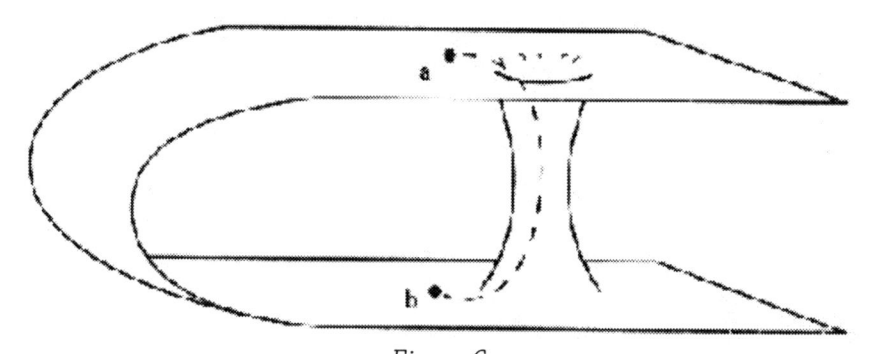

Figure 6
Shortcut through space. If the space in Figure 5 above is folded over, the wormhole straightens out and is more suggestive of a shorter route between **a** *and* **b**. *Illustrations by Timothy Ferris, The Whole Shebang (New York, 1977) Page 246, 247.*

Wormholes could provide the ultimate in efficient travel. A wormhole a mile long might connect two regions of space hundreds of light-years apart. If we could dive into the mouth of a wormhole and survive the trip, we would emerge from the other end to find ourselves in a remote sector of the universe, having traveled a vast distance in little or no time. Their assumed ability to transport space travelers millions of light-years in an instant has made wormholes a feature of science fiction novels whose plots demand an intergalactic rapid-transit system. (See Figure 5)

If blackholes have taught science anything it is that one should not reject a promising idea solely because it leads to bizarre conclusions. So we may wish to be reticent about rejecting wormhole speculations out of hand, even though they point toward conclusions so strange as to make blackholes seem familiar as old shoes.

Kip Thorne (1994) writes, in his book on blackholes and time warps, that it might be possible to hold wormholes open in such a way as to make them accommodating to travelers. The Thorne conjecture raised the possibility that wormholes could be used as time machines, capable of transporting wormhole travelers not only across space, but through time, into the past. This prospect aroused so much attention from the press that Thorne stopped using the phrase, "time travel" in his papers, replacing it with a technical synonym, "closed time like loops," which few journalists understood and few, therefore, wrote about.

Traveling into the past of one's own universe violates causality and thus creates severe paradoxes. If you climbed into a wormhole in your living room and returned one minute earlier than you had departed, you would not only have created a copy of yourself but you could stop yourself from climbing into the wormhole, in which case the version of yourself that stopped yourself would not have shown up to intervene! Many physicists believe time travel to be literally impossible (Ferris, 1997).

Ferris writes that there are two arenas in which we can imagine time travel taking place without violating causality. Both involve locations separated from our universe.

One notion is that wormholes connect not one region of our universe to another but a place in our universe to a place in another universe. The other suggests that time travel can indeed take place - but only inside blackholes. A blackhole is defined as a collapsed star or other object with a gravitational field so intense that its escape velocity exceeds that of light. Blackholes are defined as objects with gravitational fields so intense that light cannot escape them. On Earth it amounts to 24,000 miles per hour, the speed that Apollo spacecraft had to exceed to carry astronauts to the moon.

The term "wormhole" was also coined by John Wheeler. In the 1950s, Wheeler envisaged the possibility that two points in space might be connectable by more than one route. The original idea is shown in Figure 5, which represents space in terms of a two-dimensional sheet. A and B are two points in space. To get from A to B by normal means, you would follow the dotted path. But there might exist a tunnel or tube (the wormhole) providing an alternative route (the dashed line). The possibility of two routes connecting the same points in space is another example of how, in general relativity, space-time may be bent around far enough to reconnect with itself, thus providing the possibility of loops in both space and time (Davies, 1995).

This is made more plausible if the diagram is folded over, as shown in Figure 6, where the wormhole now appears as a short tube. Einstein anticipated this type of geometry in work carried out with Nathan Rosen in the mid-1930s. For that reason, a wormhole is sometimes known as an "Einstein-Rosen bridge." It may happen that an astronaut can get from A to B through the wormhole faster than light can get there via the "normal" route. By outpacing light in this manner, the astronaut can also travel backwards in time.

Frustrated by the seemingly insurmountable barrier presented by the speed of light, scientists interested in the UFO phenomenon have come up with what they see as alternative origins for the alien visitors. According to Einstein's theories, for example, any object that accelerates toward the speed of light undergoes a bizarre transformation. Not only does its mass increase, but its volume shrinks and its own rate of time slows toward zero. Hypothetically, if an object could reach the light-speed barrier, time would have stopped altogether, and the object - now infinitely small, and infinitely heavy - could be said to vanish. In theory, at least, it drops out of our familiar space-time universe. And where does it go? The answer, according to ufologist Michael Swords, editor of Journal of UFO Studies, may be that it pops up in another universe, composed of other dimensions (Flaherty, 1992).

For those who believe UFOs are indeed crewed by interstellar travelers, this might provide a cosmic shortcut for alien space pilots, who could speed through the barrier of the present universe, then emerge an instant later in the vicinity of Earth. But Swords speculates there are other possibilities as well. If time dwindles to zero at the critical moment, it could show up on the other side as a mathematical negative. In effect, it would run backward. This suggests to Swords that alien astronauts may be travelers from the future, who have come back to present-day Earth in order to recapture their own past, and perhaps to change the course of history for the better.

At the beginning of this century, Albert Einstein added time as a fourth dimension. Since then, theoretical scientists attempting to describe the structure and behavior of our universe have devised mathematical formulas that call for even more dimensions, some of which are "folded inside" others.

No ufologist doubts that the research into every aspect of this complex phenomenon should continue, for the UFO puzzle shows no signs of imminent solution. The key for those who would unravel the mystery is to approach each investigation in a dispassionate, scientific manner, unclouded by prejudice or emotional bias. It is imperative that we keep an open mind about these things.

DIRECT CONFRONTATION

Scientists ask the question, "How will mankind react when a direct confrontation between man and extraterrestrial intelligence occurs?" All we have to do is turn on the television set and we can hear actual stories of these encounters from regular folks who claim that they have indeed had direct confrontations with Extraterrestrial Biological Entities. Some claim that their life goes on as usual with very little change in their psyche. Some claim a tremendous responsibility to carry the news of this experience throughout the world; to educate, to share, to inform and to enlighten. This information sharing and these experiences have not been widely accepted. Man appears to be apprehensive when it comes to losing his place in the intellectual hierarchy.

Man is so completely accustomed to regarding himself as supreme that to discover he is no more an intellectual match for beings elsewhere than our dogs are for us would be a shattering revelation (Sullivan, 1993). Carl Gustav Jung, the disciple of Freud, said of a direct confrontation with such creatures: The "reins would be torn from our hands and we would find ourselves without dreams, that is, we would find our intellectual and spiritual aspirations so outmoded as to leave us completely paralyzed." Jung should have lived long enough to have met me! Myself, as well as others, have not been paralyzed by our new belief systems concerning extraterrestrials.

The SETI pioneer, Frank Drake is among those who believe that inhabitants of other worlds are immortal. He wrote that when we first discover other civilizations in space we will be the dumbest of them all, and probably the only mortal civilization. Carl Sagan has discussed the possibility that the inhabitants of other worlds might not only have become immortal but lost all motivation for "interstellar gallivanting." He surely was not thinking about rogues, now was he?

PARADIGM SHIFT

Believers still maintain that UFOs are physically real, solid metallic-like craft piloted by superior creatures who, through their mastery of some form of advanced system of propulsion, are able to transport themselves through space from their galaxy to ours at velocities that defy the physical laws of the universe as we understand them.

Skeptics still say it's all hogwash. The immutable laws of physics dictate no material object can approach the speed of light; therefore, because of the vastness of our universe, no extraterrestrial beings could reach us without traveling tens of thousands of Earth years to get here (Bryan 1995).

The advent of the abduction phenomenon has served only to enlarge the debate to include such technological riddles as: How are these alien beings able to levitate people up beams of light? How do they communicate telepathically? In short, "What is going on?" and "What do they want from us?" have been added to "Where are they from?"

UFOlogists have theorized that some of the mysterious objects may come from some other dimension and are therefore not from some planet in "outer space."

It has been suggested that alien space craft do not travel through space as we know it but through dimensions of consciousness, that they are in contact with intelligences far removed from us and that they can travel anywhere with the speed of thought (Steiger & White, 1975).

In his "Mysteries of Time and Space" Brad Steiger theorizes that UFOs may posses a kind of intelligence that enables them to influence our minds telepathically and to project what appear to be three-dimensional images to the observers of UFO activity. In other words, there may be no spacecraft, there may be no UFO occupants - there may be only glowing globs of pure intelligence, permitting each observer to view them in a manner that would be most acceptable to them (Steiger, 1974).

That may be why some UFO observers report a confrontation with beautiful, long-haired, human-like entities; some with bug-eyed monsters; others with small, gray astronaut-type aliens. The changing shapes reported by observers of flying saucers throughout the world have been: a wheel, a globe, a cigar shape, a fireball, and so forth. It may all depend upon what preconceptions the observer might have about alien lifeforms.

It is the opinion of some UFOlogists that external intelligence has been interacting with mankind in an effort to learn more about us or in an effort to communicate certain concepts to us. It appears that there is a definite symbiotic relationship which exists between man and the UFO intelligences. In some manner we do not yet understand, they need us as much as we need them. The best teachers are those who bring their eager, but sometimes silly and protesting, students just short of the solution to a problem, then step aside to permit the awkward students themselves the sense of accomplishment to be found in having solved a seemingly impossible riddle.

Whatever the guise these intelligences assume, it would seem that they have interacted with mankind on a very subtle level for centuries.

WORLD VIEW

In June of 1992, a scientific conference was held at the Massachusetts Institute of Technology (MIT) to assess the similarities and differences in the findings of various investigators studying people who report experiences of abductions by aliens, and the related issues of this phenomenon. The five day conference was co-chaired by John E. Mack, M.D., cum laude graduate of the Harvard Medical School, where he has been a professor of psychiatry for the past twenty years (Bryan, 1995).

In Dr. Mack's presentation at the conference he stated that a shift in our world-view is needed. He went on to say that our belief system is based on the existence of a physical world. We see music, art, etc., as being in the spirit world, but are they real? The alien abduction phenomenon attacks our perception of reality, and speaks of alien beings who float through walls and turn on and off television sets as a way of showing off their technological superiority. Is it an intrusion into our space or some sort of psychic phenomenon? Our materialist concept requires that we choose: are they in the spirit world, or are they in the real world? This way of thinking forces us to learn, to expand our notions of reality. What it means is that we must rethink our whole place in the cosmos. What we need to do is open our consciousness.

Conscious acknowledgment of these experiences, looking at them squarely and confronting your fears about it, effects a transformative change in your life. It usually changes forever how you perceive your reality. At that point, you undergo a paradigm shift.

If we accept the possibility that these Beings, whatever form they may take, have been in contact with us for tens of thousands of years, then we should not discard the possibility that we may very well be something different from what we believe ourselves to be, on this earth for reasons that may not yet be known to us, the understanding of which will be an immense challenge. The least demanding "shift in worldview" required by this phenomenon asks only that we extend those boundaries that we deem to be the limits of technology. In other words, just because UFOs and their occupants defy our laws of physics does not mean there are not further laws of physics we have not as yet discovered or do not as yet comprehend. Technology is constantly advancing; stunning scientific achievements, therefore, should not surprise us (Bryan, 1995).

Some believe that the paradigm shift required by acknowledging that there might be other intelligent beings in the universe will set us back on our heels. Is there a government conspiracy to prevent the public from learning more about the UFO phenomenon? Will there be fear over our inability to cope with the fact that our government is not able to protect our skies. And would a government readily admit this fact to the public? Will this render us totally helpless? Would people panic? And if it is acknowledged as real can you then deny it exists? Therefore, you can not acknowledge it. You have to deny it. You not only have to deny the existence of these paranormal events but you also have to block people's access to what information they do have, which is what creates the sense of a conspiracy.

Who decides what is real in a given culture? It's really a very small percentage of the population who determines this. It's similar to when the church took over from the pagan beliefs of Europe. Although the Church became the official religion, the people went on believing whatever they had believed privately. It's sort of like that now. Seventy to eighty percent of the people may believe in UFOs, but the military and scientific community says they don't exist. So they don't exist.

FINAL THOUGHTS

In my interview with Jesse Marcel, one of the things I wanted to know was if a paradigm shift had taken place in his reality due to the incident at Roswell. Looking back, I think it did.

As far back as 1947, he believed that there were other intelligent beings in the universe and that there was a government conspiracy to prevent the public from learning more about the UFO phenomenon. He believed that there was a technology that could run circles around any technology that we had. He may have assisted the government in their denial of the existence of these paranormal events but in the end he came forward and told the public what he knew.

Jesse left this physical world and I'd like to think that he has traveled to that strange world from which the extraterrestrials seem to emanate. I expect to see him there.

If we accept the possibility that Extraterrestrial Beings have been in contact with us, then we should not discard the possibility that we may very well be something different from what we believe ourselves to be. Therefore, I believe that we are on this earth for reasons that are not yet known to us.

Conscious acknowledgment of these experiences, looking at them squarely and confronting our fears about it, effects a transformative change in our life. It usually changes forever how we perceive our reality. At that point, we undergo a paradigm shift; possibly with a great deal of resistance.

Resistance has to do with the fact that a culture becomes deeply committed to a point of view, a way of seeing the world. And we've cut ourselves off from so much of the spirit world. We are not attuned to anything other than that which shows up in conventional physical reality, because we don't have the sense to know anything else. We've lost those senses and have paid such a price for being masters of the physical universe. Our senses have atrophied. Those senses through which every people, including us before the Seventeenth Century, have known. We no longer sense the Spirit realities, realities beyond the material world.

Whitley Strieber writes that, "The visitors represent the most powerful of all forces acting in human culture. They may be extraterrestrials managing the evolution of the human mind. Or they may represent the presence of mind on another level of being. Perhaps our fate is eventually to leave the physical world altogether and join them in that strange hyper-reality from which they seem to emerge."

THE END

BIBLIOGRAPHY

Asimov, Isaac. 1981. Asimov's Guide to the Bible. NY: Avenel.
Asimov, Isaac. 1982. Exploring the Earth and the Cosmos. NY: Crown Publishers.
Berliner, Barbara. 1990. The Book of Answers. NY: The Stonesong Press, Inc.
Berlitz, Charles, & Moore, William L. 1980. The Roswell Incident. NY: Berkley Books.
Bernstein, Jeremy. 1963. The Analytical Engine: Computers Past, Present, and Future. NY: Random House.
Bradlaugh, Charles. 1967. In Paul Edwards, "Atheism." The Encyclopedia of Philosophy. NY: Macmillan. Vol. 1.
Bryan, C. D. B. 1995. Close Encounters of the Fourth Kind: Alien Abductions, UFOs, and the Conference at MIT NY: Alfred A. Knopf.
Claiborne, Robert. 1974. The Birth of Writing. NY: Time Life Books.
Constable, George. 1987. The Age of God-Kings. Virginia: Time Life Books.
Davies, Paul. 1995. About Time: Einstein's Unfinished Revolution. NY: Simon & Schuster.
Dewey, Edward. 1971. Cycles: The Mysterious Forces That Trigger Events. NY: Hawthorn Books.
Diringer, David. 1968. The Alphabet: A Key to the History of Mankind. NY: Funk & Wagnalls.
Eiseley, Loren. 1978. The Star-Thrower. NY: Time Books.
Eliot, T. S. 1943. Four Quartets: Little Gidding. Part 5 NY: Harcourt,

Brace & Company.
Evans, J. 1979. The Mystery of the Pyramids. NY: Crown.
Ferris, Timothy. 1997. The Whole Shebang. NY: Simon & Schuster.
Friedman, Louis D. 1997. The Planetary Society Newsletter.
Jensen, Hans. 1969. Sign, Symbol and Script. NY: G.P. Putnam's Sons.
Mertz, Barbara. 1964. Temples, Tombs and Hieroglyphs. NY: Dodd, Mead & CO. Inc.
Moore, Dan, & Waller, Martha. 1962. Cloak & Cipher. NY: The Bobbs-Merrill CO. Inc.
Newby, P. H., and Maroon, Fred J. 1979. The Egypt Story. NY: Abbeville Press, Inc.
Russell, Bertrand. 1986. In John D. Barrow & Frank Tipler. The Anthropic Cosmological Principle. Oxford: Oxford University Press.
Sagan, Carl, & Druyan, Ann. 1992. Shadows of Forgotten Ancestors: A Search for Who We Are. NY: Random House.
Scott, Joseph and Lenore. 1968. Egyptian Hieroglyphs for Everyone. NY: Funk & Wagnalls Publishing Co. Inc.
Shklovskii, I. S. & Sagan, Carl. 1966. Intelligent Life In The Universe. San Francisco: Holden Day, Inc.
Sitchin, Zecharia. 1980. The Stairway To Heaven. NY: St. Martin's Press.
Solomon, Robert C. & Higgens, Kathleen M. 1996. A Short History of Philosophy. NY: Oxford University Press.
Steiger, Brad. 1974. Mysteries of Time and Space. NY: Dell Publishing Co.
Steiger, Brad, & White, John. 1975. Other Worlds, Other Universes: Playing The Reality Game. MY: Doubleday & Company.
Strieber, W. 1988. Transformation: The Breakthrough. NY: William Morrow & Co.
Sullivan, Walter. 1993. We Are Not Alone. NY: Dutton Books.
Thorne, Kip S. 1994. Black Holes and Time Warps. NY: Norton.
von Daniken, Erich. 1970. Gods From Outer Space. NY: G. P. Putnam's Sons.
Wrixon, Fred B. 1989. Codes, Ciphers, and Secret Languages. NY: Bonanza Books.

Printed in the United States
70052LV00003B/82-129